Getting Along: Teaching Social Skills to Children and Youth

D1568307

Getting Along: Teaching Social Skills to Children and Youth

by Jim Ollhoff and Laurie Ollhoff

Sparrow Media Group, Inc.
Farmington, MN

Printed and bound in the United States.
Second Printing
First edition, 2004.

Content Editor: Karen Washington
Content Editor: Joshua Koepp

Quantity discounts are available for organizations or universities. Contact:
Sparrow Media Group
16588 Fieldcrest Avenue, Farmington, MN 55024
952-953-9166
info@sparrowmediagroup.com
www.sparrowmediagroup.com

Library of Congress Cataloging-in-Publication Data

Ollhoff, Jim, 1959-
   Getting along : teaching social skills to children and youth / Jim Ollhoff,
Laurie Ollhoff.
     p. cm.
   Includes index.
   ISBN 978-0-9786018-7-4
   1. Social skills in children--Study and teaching. 2. Interpersonal relations in
children--Study and teaching. 3. Social interaction in children--Study and
teaching. 4. Life skills--Study and teaching. I. Ollhoff, Laurie. II. Title.

HQ783.O54 2007
372.82--dc22
                                    2007008708

Table of Contents

Case Studies

Tables and Charts

Introduction

"Without friends no one would choose to live, though he had all other goods."
—Aristotle, 384-322 BC

LITTLE JOEY, a 1st grader, consistently plays too rough. His games with other children often result in some kind of physical violence. Many of the children don't want to play with Joey anymore. When he gets frustrated, he throws books or pencils or tries to break something. During outside free time, Joey always recruits some of the other boys for a martial arts "kick-em-sock-em-smash-em" role play.

Sarah rarely makes eye contact with anyone. She always does what the staff ask of her, but she doesn't talk much. Sarah's face is always turned toward the floor. Without many friends, she frequently plays by herself and never shows interest in new games. She shies away from any new experiences.

Children need a wide variety of social skills to live peacefully, assertively, and calmly.

Some of the staff call Jacob "competitive." But it is more than that. When Jacob loses a game, he cries, argues, or lies about the outcome. In the gym, Jacob is intense and fiery, screaming at his teammates who make mistakes. Every game is a contest, and every contest seems to be a life or death struggle for Jacob. No one has ever seen Jacob laugh.

The stories of Joey, Sarah, and Jacob are all too common. Each lacks some kind of social skill. Without those skills, Joey, Sarah and Jacob will not likely succeed in life. Children need a wide variety of social skills to live peacefully, assertively, and calmly.

There was a time, not too long ago, when our social structures included extended family and strong communities where there existed naturally occurring opportunities for social skill development. However, those natural "social skill builders" are no longer in place. As society has evolved, few children have the experiences of heavy adult interaction and mentoring by older children that were a normal part of ages past. Because those opportunities no longer exist, adults must now intentionally teach social skills. The good news is that it is fairly easy to teach kids social skills–but it doesn't "just kind of happen"! Today, for children to learn social skills, adults need to think about it, plan for it, be intentional about it, and work on it.

School-age programs are one of the few places with all the factors necessary for teaching social skills. Typically these out-of-school-time programs include children of all ages, have a spirit of community, and have naturally occurring social situations from which children can learn. School-age out-of-school-time programs might be the most effective places in the child's life to teach those peaceful living skills.

In fact, we view the role of school-age care providers as "teachers of social skills." They are not the *only* social skill teachers, of course, but they are important ones. The role of the school-age care provider is not to just supervise children or simply keep kids safe. *The role of the school-age care provider is to teach social skills.*

The first section of this book discusses the need to teach social skills to children. It discusses the "whys" of teaching social skills, and some of the societal issues that make teaching social skills a critical part of children's development.

The second section of the book examines the social skills themselves, breaking them down into seven skill clusters. The categorizing of social skills is a helpful way to think through kids' needs.

> **The role of the school-age care provider is to teach social skills.**

The third section of the book explains the three ways to teach social skills. For maximum effectiveness, all three methods should be a part of any social skill training program.

A school-age care provider is a facilitator of positive development. We are part of the village that raises the child. It is important for us to know something about imparting and communicating those peaceful living skills. The viability of our global village depends on those values and skills.

Jim Ollhoff
Laurie Ollhoff

SOCIAL SKILLS

Overview of Social Skills

In this chapter:

❖ The definition of social skills
❖ Categorizing social skills into seven clusters
❖ How social skills build on one another

Chapter 1
What Are
Social Skills?

"A friend might well be reckoned the masterpiece of nature."
—Ralph Waldo Emerson, 1803-1882

SOCIAL SKILLS are the skills with which we interact with others. It's all the verbal and nonverbal tasks and expressions that we use to live with others.

Some of those skills are used in direct contact with other people—such as communication, listening, and making friends. Some skills are tasks such as helping others, caring for animals, or dealing with emergencies.

Some skills are expressed largely to ourselves, such as how we deal with stress or how confident we are in ourselves. These are called "social skills" because the ways we feel about ourselves are shaped by the interactions we have with others—and, the interactions we have with others shape how we feel about ourselves. So, skills such as *being curious, having self-esteem,* and *having a sense that we are loved and valued* are also under the umbrella of social skills.

Using our Skills for Good

A person can have a lot of skills, or a few skills. We can perform a particular skill very robustly, or very poorly. An attentive adult can observe the child's interactions and get a sense of the skills they have, and what skills need more work. An adult working with children can assess the children's social skills, for the purpose of helping them learn the necessary skills.

The point of watching children is not to judge them! The point is to watch and assess their social skill level so that we might teach them appropriate skills. If all we did is assess their social skills, and then at the end of the week, tell the parents, "Timmy has lousy self-esteem," we would be using this knowledge unethically. If we believe Timmy has low self-esteem, we can design simple activities and engage in intentional interactions directed at increasing that skill.

When teachers begin to teach a new subject, they typically assess children's knowledge of the subject so they can teach more effectively. That's what we must do with social skills—we must assess their social skills, to ensure that our teaching and guidance can be most effective.

Too often, when a child shows poor social skills, adults remove them from the very situations where the child could practice the skill. We can make the social skill problems worse by continuing to remove the child from the social environments where they could learn appropriateness. For example, let's say a group of children are playing a board game, and are having repeated arguments about whose turn it is and what the cards mean. As the children get louder, the adults says, "Since this game is making you fight, I think we'll put it away for the rest of the week." The adult just missed an opportunity to teach the skills that the children need to learn!

Of course, in some extreme behavior issues, children must be removed—at least temporarily. But if we never teach children the appropriate way to interact with each other, we may find ourselves frustrated because "those kids never act in the appropriate way with each other." We need to teach skills and allow them to practice the appropriate skills.

Figure #1: Social Skills List

Reflect back on your experience with school-age children and youth. What were the social skills issues that showed up as the greatest area of need?

A sense of feeling capable	Communication	Non-competitiveness
A sense of humor	Conflict resolution	Playfulness
A sense of significance	Cooperation	Problem-solving
Accepting consequences	Coping with stress	Relaxing
Assertiveness	Dealing with anger	Respecting others
Behaving appropriately	Empathy	Responsibility
Being Fair	Ethical behavior	Self-awareness
Being independent of peer pressure	Following through	Self-control
Caring for the environment	Helping others	Self-esteem
	Making friends	Setting goals
	Listening	Sharing
	Making wise choices	Understanding others
	Negotiation	

Clustering the Skills

There are many ways to categorize and organize social skills. This book will use a method called *The Seven Cs*. This list separates all the social skills into seven categories, or skill-sets.

Confidence: having a sense of being loved and being capable
Control: having an inner locus of control
Coping: dealing with negative emotions and circumstances
Curiosity: having a sense of wonderment about the world.
Communication: being able to listen and express oneself
Community Building: making friends
Conflict Resolution: working through conflict toward resolution

The first four skills (confidence, control, coping, and curiosity) can be called *intrapersonal social skills*. *Intrapersonal* means "within oneself." While these skills are birthed and shaped through our interactions with others, they are used within oneself. The next three skills (communication, community building, and conflict resolution) are called *interpersonal skills*, because they are typically used in connection and interactions with others.

Figure #2: The Seven Cs Social Skill Clusters

Intrapersonal Skills   Interpersonal skills

Confidence   *Communication*
Self-esteem   Expressing feelings
Sense of feeling capable   Speaking
Sense of being loved   Listening
Belief in one's abilities   Assertiveness

Control   *Community Building*
Internal locus of control   Friendship skills
Self-discipline   Working in groups
Responsibility   Cooperation
Impulse control   Empathy

Coping   *Conflict Resolution*
Dealing with stress   Distaste for violence
Anger management   Values the resolution process
Dealing with crisis   Can think of solutions
Feeling calm in chaotic times   Negotiation

Curiosity
Intrinsic motivation
Desire to learn new things
Desire to explore and create
adventure
Sense of humor

The Pyramid Approach

One approach to The Seven Cs is to view them as a pyramid, with "higher" skills being dependent on the foundation of "lower" skills.

Figure #3: The Pyramid Approach to The Seven Cs

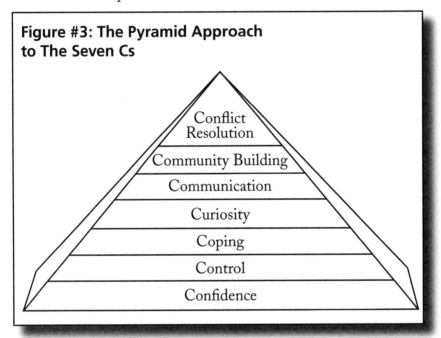

The idea behind this approach is that each skill cluster is built on the preceding skill. This means that healthy confidence is necessary for control. Similarly, confidence and control skills help a child develop healthy coping skills. Confidence, control, and coping are also essential for developing curiosity, communication, and community-building.

In other words, it isn't very effective to teach conflict resolution skills to children who don't value each other (community building). It isn't very effective to teach children how to be curious when they are afraid of trying new things (confidence). It isn't very effective to teach community-building to children who don't have the skills to listen or converse (communication). The pyramid approach suggests that if you want to teach curiosity, you will get a bigger bang for your buck if you make sure the skills of coping, control, and confidence are in place.

As you assess social skills (see chapter 11), you can use the pyramid as a map. If you find you need to improve both communication and conflict resolution, look at the pyramid, and start with the lower one (communication). Work on communication first, *then* work on the skills of conflict resolution.

Social Skills in Out-of-School Time Settings

Programs that serve children and youth during out-of-school time have the opportunity and responsibility to support growth and learning of social skills.

In fact, there isn't much choice in the matter. Children will aquire skills whether we want them to or not. The question is, *will they pick up positive skills or negative skills?* If we are intentional about what we teach, the children will be much better off in the long run. Adults who work with children have the responsibility to cultivate the program to support the healthy development of social skills. The flexible schedule allows structured teaching of social skills. The unregimented time allows flexibility for grabbing the teachable moment and following through with the one-on-one coaching needed to generalize the skill into new situations.

When school-age care providers create the opportunities to teach and support the growth and development of social skills, children will gain the skills they need for a lifetime. The benefits of the learning are immediate. Children will experience closer and deeper friendships. They will possess the skills to de-stress themselves and to handle life experiences with a positive outlook. With the building blocks of the 7C's in place, children and youth will have the opportunity to grow into competent, confident, caring, and contributing adults.

Here's the Point

The 7Cs are the developmental tasks of childhood. As we engage children through our program design, we have the opportunity to be intentional about what we teach. When we teach—through our nurturing, our discipline, and our program design—we can set children up for success by working for positive development of social skills.

Case Study #1: Mr. Bluto and Ms. Vickie

Mr. Bluto is the Lead Coordinator for the school-age program. In the spring, he attended several workshops on conflict resolution, and felt he was becoming an expert on the topic. When the summer school-age program began, he spent the first two weeks, four hours a day, teaching the children conflict resolution techniques. He invited speakers, made the kids practice, gave mini-lectures, played conflict-resolution games, performed role plays, sang conflict resolution songs, etc. The children seemed bored and unengaged most of the time. And when the two weeks were done, Mr. Bluto did not see any increased activity in conflict resolution, nor did he see any increase in community. Most of the children still did not know one another's names, many children still sat alone, and arguments and fights were never resolved.

Ms. Vickie, at the school-age program down the street, assessed her children at the beginning of summer. Many of the children were new, and many children had no friends in the program. Ms. Vickie spent the first two weeks playing games and conducting activities designed to help the children to get to know one another. By the end of the two weeks, all the children knew everyone's names, many friendships were forming, and few children played alone. As the interactions became more common, the natural consequence, of course, were more conflicts. During the third and fourth week, Ms. Vickie conducted an intensive effort to teach conflict resolution. After the conflict-resolution training, the conflict-resolution sofa was frequently occupied, and there was a noticeable drop in arguments that escalated into fights.

Frequently Asked Questions

Q What can providers do to ensure that they are taking a good approach to social skill building?

A In a way, social-skill building is a little like exercising: Anything is better than nothing. You don't need a lot of extra training, you don't need to read a stack of books, and you don't need a college degree (but none of those things hurt!). You can start teaching social skills by simply observing children's interaction carefully, and starting with small steps.

Q What research is being conducted on the best practices for teaching social skills?

A Research is being conducted on every aspect of social skills. Originally, the research started in the area of handicapped children, and then spread into juvenile delinquent populations, and then "normal" children. A good summary of the research can be found in Cartledge, G. & Milburn, J.F. (1995). *Teaching social skills to children and youth: Innovative approaches.* Needham Heights, MA: Allyn and Bacon.

Q How should SAC providers approach social skill building with parents?

A Providers can and should be upfront with parents about their schedules, themes, and teachings. So, you might want to let parents know that "we'll be doing some self-esteem exercises this month," or "we're practicing good communication this week." Parents should always have the freedom to discuss the theme or specific exercises.

Discussion Questions

1. Which skill listed in Figure 1 do you think is most important? Why?
2. Reflect on one of the Seven Cs. Where did you learn this particular skill? Which adults or peers in your life helped you develop that skill?
3. What are some of the consequences of a lack of social skills? What behavior will you see in a child in the 3rd grade, 6th grade, or 12th grade who lacks a particular social skill? What behavior will you see in an adult who lacks a particular social skill?
4. What changes do you think have happened in the socialization process for children, that makes the development of social skills less "natural"?
5. What are the dangers for adults who watch social skills? What might be some of the unethical behavior in which an adult could engage?
6. What's the difference between the approaches of Mr. Bluto and Ms. Vickie (Case #1)? What were Mr. Bluto's mistakes? What will Ms. Vickie have to do to continue her success?

Helpful Readings

Coloroso, B. (2002). *School-age children are worth it: Giving your child the gift of inner discipline.* New York: HarperResources.

Glenn, S.H. (2000). *Raising self-reliant children in a self-indulgent world.* Rocklin, CA: Prima Publishing.

Reference Notes

- The 7Cs were developed by Jim Ollhoff. The Pyramid Approach was developed by Laurie Ollhoff.
- Some of the classic works in the field of social skill building are:
  - Alberg, J., Petry, C., & Eller, S. (1994). *Social skills planning guide.* Longmont, CO: Sopris West.
  - Combs, M.L., & Slaby, D.A. (1977). *Social skills training with children.* In B.B. Lahey and A.E. Kazdin (Eds.), Advances in clinical child psychology, Volume 1. New York: Plenum Press.
  - Duck, S. (1991). *Understanding relationships.* New York: Guilford Press.
  - Elkind, D. (1994). *Ties that stress: The new family imbalance.* Cambridge, MA: Harvard University Press.
  - Greenspan, S. (1993). *Playground politics: Understanding the emotional life of your school-age child.* Reading, MA: Addison-Wesley Publishing Company.

In this chapter:

- ❖ In the old days, children learned social skills naturally as they grew up
- ❖ What happens when kids have low social skills
- ❖ The best places to teach social skills

Chapter 2
Why Teach
Social Skills?

*"The worst solitude is to be destitute of
sincere friendship."*
—Sir Francis Bacon, 1561-1626

LEARNING SOCIAL SKILLS used to be
a natural part of the socialization process. A
generation ago, school-age children learned social
skills naturally. It was simply part of growing up.

Children had to learn negotiation skills when
six siblings were sleeping in one bed. Children
had to learn sharing when there were only
hand-me-downs to wear. Children had to learn
responsibility when it was their job to milk the
cows in the morning (if they forgot, no one had
milk). Children learned maturity from the three-
and-a-half hours they spent doing chores with an
adult every day. Older children learned skills of
helping when they helped the younger children
with homework in the one-room schoolhouse.

Society was set up in a way that helped
children learn social skills as they moved
through life. Today that is no longer true. Most
mechanisms that helped facilitate social skills
are gone. The extended family is gone. Time
with adults is minimal and superficial. Instead
of interaction, we have television. Instead of
mentoring, we have video games.

Certainly, we don't mean to create an unrealistically rosy picture of the "good ole days." There were things happening in the "good ole days" that were abominable. There are many advantages of living in today's families.

So what was once a natural part of the socialization process must now be taught intentionally.

However, let's just examine that narrow slice of life: how children learned social skills. When we look at that, we find that children used to learn social skills as a part of growing up. They don't anymore.

So what was once a natural part of the socialization process must now be taught intentionally.

The Threads of Socialization

The socialization process has had three main threads—the places where kids spend their time:

1) Family Time
2) School Time
3) Time outside of the school and not with family—what we call *Childhood Time.*

Children of this generation have experienced huge changes in the Family Time, as compared with previous generations (for example, the loss of the extended family).

But there have also been huge changes in Childhood Time. Children are exposed to far more than previous generations—on television, in popular music, and the Internet. There are no limits to what children may see—the boundaries that used to exist seem null and void in an era of the Internet, cable, and digital television. Most children are bombarded with images of sex, violence, and adult situations before they have the skills to sort them out rationally. We have a generation of children who are sophisticated before they are mature.

Other changes have had a physical impact on childhood such as a change in diet—more fast and convenient foods—accompanied by a decline in activity (due to television and video games). Children have a much higher incidence of diabetes and obesity than previous generations. Further, children have quicker access to illegal drugs and alcohol than in the past.

Let's Blame Someone!

As society sees children becoming in-risk and at-risk in greater numbers, there is a frantic search for causes. Much of the knee-jerk, arm-chair blaming has fallen on the school.

Educational reformists have, of course, seen the problem of rising at-risk behavior and low social skills of children and youth. Many of these reformists have tried to address the problem by lengthening the school day, creating year-round school, or by requiring classroom teachers to teach social skills as another subject. Education is under the spotlight for a problem of at-risk behavior of children and youth—a problem that they did not cause, and a problem they cannot fix on their own.

Our partners in the classroom cannot fix the problem of at-riskness by themselves. Quality school-age care programs can be powerful components of kids' positive development. It is in the out-of-school time environments where natural social situations—so important for teaching social skills—exist.

The good news for kids is that, with a little bit of intentionality, and a little bit of knowledge, it's fairly easy to teach kids social skills. And kids benefit greatly from that learning. The research evidence for its effectiveness as well as the illustrative stories of its success continues to grow.

The Costs of Inadequate Social Skills

Kids and Guns. Every day 135,000 students carry guns to school. On average 20% of youth, grades 9-12, carried a weapon in the last month. Over 7% of high school students were threatened or injured with a weapon on school property during the last 12 months.

Alcohol-related deaths. More than one-third of high school students reported that, in the last month, they had ridden with a driver who had been drinking.

Teenage sex and pregnancy. Thirteen percent of all U.S. births are to teenagers. Eight percent of high school girls report date rape.

Deaths and injuries from conflict. Forty percent of teenage girls know someone their age who has been hit or beaten by a boyfriend.

Abuse. Almost a million children were abused or neglected this year. Of course, tragically, this is only the number of children that were *reported* to be abused. The unreported number of abused children is much higher.

Suicide. Suicide is the third leading cause of death among young people aged 15-24. Five thousand teenagers commit suicide each year, and there are 30-50 times as many teenagers attempt suicide.

Influence of TV. Thirty years of research on television suggests that children who watch a lot of TV are more likely to exhibit a lack of social skills, poor self-esteem, more interpersonal conflict, more violence, and poorer cognitive abilities. No doubt this is a combination of violent images and the lack of human interaction. Certainly, this is a factor in the loss of social skills as well as part of the cost of social skills.

Overall, about 50,000 children and youth die each year because of low social skills—through suicides, runaways, fatal conflicts, drug overdoses, etc. Countless more are scarred or put on the road of permanent negative development.

The Best Places to Teach Social Skills

School-age care programs will never be as good at teaching curricular subjects as schools. However, schools will never be as good at teaching social skills as the child care programs.

Schools have difficulty teaching social skills for a variety of reasons:

- Teachers might not have the expertise.
- Schedules in schools are highly structured.
- Children sit in rows with little chance to interact.
- Children in classes are all the same age.
- Teachers are often regimented by legislatures to teach subjects for a certain number of minutes per subject per day.
- The fixation on standardized tests creates more pressure in schools to focus on academics.

Some school-age programs might give up teaching social skills to spend more time on homework and teaching time. However, doing the same things they do in school may not meet the children's needs. The irony is, that when children are taught social skills, their grades improve! This shouldn't surprise us, since brain research informs us that stress and threat get the brain ready to fight or flee, not learn. Social skills enable children to more effectively manage stress and threat.

The perfect environment for teaching social skills has four components:

- A lot of adult-child interaction. Adults and children need to be able to rub elbows frequently, so that adults can take opportunities to teach social skills.
- A high degree of play and spontaneity. The best time to reinforce the skills of conflict resolution is when kids are having a conflict! When the environment has play and spontaneity, kids will need to practice their social skills (and, the lack of social skills becomes more apparent).
- A multi-aged environment. Children need to be taught and skills need to be reinforced by children who are older and more mature. This kind of mentoring not only helps the "mentee," but also teaches the mentor important skills!
- Adults who are attentive to children's social needs. The adults don't need a ton of knowledge to begin teaching social skills. They simply need to be good observers and be attentive to children.

Teaching Social Skills in School-Age Care

School-age care is a multi-aged, grouped, relatively unstructured time. In quality programs, the staff work with the children to develop a program that is responsive to the developmental needs of children and youth. In SAC, the staff— the facilitators of positive development—have the opportunity to use time flexibly, and to allow for children to explore, dabble, mingle, mix, dialog, and interact. School-age care is a place where children must practice the skills of getting along with others.

School-age care is a place where children must practice the skills of getting along with others.

The flexible schedule allows for both structured and unstructured teaching of social skills. The unregimented time allows for the flexibility to grab the teachable moment, following through with the one-on-one coaching needed to generalize the skill into new situations. Taking advantage of the teachable moment is the best way to help children see that social skills can be used in real-life situations.

After World War II, families moved away from their extended family. In doing so, children lost that important resource for learning social skills. However, school-age care can be the new extended family. School-age care providers can be important teachers in the children's development—particularly, learning social skills.

Here's the Point

More intentionality is required in the school-age care profession. Care providers must see themselves as facilitators of positive development and teachers of social skills. If care providers do not take the opportunity to help children on the road to positive development, we will lose tens of thousands of children in this generation.

Frequently Asked Questions

Q If we teach social skills, are we taking away the parents' responsibility?

A We aren't "taking away" anything from parents at all! We are providing an adjunct service in the same way that a pastor, teacher, coach, or police officer does. Parents will always be the best at instilling values in children. But in no society have parents ever been the *only* people to influence children. In school-age care, children are in that multi-generational environment needed to practice social skills. We help and support parents as they seek to help children on a road toward positive development.

Q Will teaching kids social skills really solve the problems that are mentioned in this chapter?

A No *one* thing will be a magic bullet to bring health and wholeness to children everywhere. However, too many children fall through the cracks because of poor social skills. As a society, we haven't done enough to help children develop these peaceful living skills—the skills of getting along. The problems mentioned previously are largely due to children and youth who don't have the social or emotional maturity to say "no" to self-destructive activities.

Discussion Questions

1. In what ways can school-age care professionals become more intentional?
2. How might your school-age care program adjust itself to be more intentional in teaching social skills?
3. How might schools get involved in your process of teaching social skills? How could families get involved in your process?
4. What other costs, besides the ones mentioned, does society pay when children have low social skills?
5. What are the changes you've seen in your lifetime, regarding Family Time, School Time, and Out-of-School Time? From what you know of your parents' or grandparents' experiences, what were those three socialization threads like for them?

Helpful Readings

Cartledge, G. & Milburn, J.F. (1995). *Teaching social skills to children and youth: Innovative approaches.* Needham Heights, MA: Allyn and Bacon.

Elkind, D. (1994). *Ties that stress: The new family imbalance.* Cambridge, MA: Harvard University Press.

Reference Notes

There are a variety of statistics in this chapter, particularly in the section "The Cost of Inadequate Social Skills." The guns statistics are taken from the Children's Defense Fund, The Center for Disease Control, and articles posted at www.crisiscounseling.com/Articles/FactsYouthViolence.htm. The information on teenage drinking is taken from the Center for Disease Control at www.cdc.gov/ncipc/factsheets/teenmvh.htm. The teenage pregnancy information was taken from the Alan Guttmacher Intstitute and Stephen Glenn's book. The information on abuse was taken from the National information clearinghouse on child abuse and neglect at www.acf.hhs.gov/programs/cb/publications/cm01/chapterone.htm#highlight. The American Psychiatric Foundation provided some of our information on suicide. The US Census bureau, at www.census.gov, gave some of the other information, along with the National Center for Children in Poverty at www.nccp.org.

Other Good Web Sites on Demographics

www.childstats.gov
www.nga.org/ National Governors Association.
www.naesp.org National Association of Elementary School Principals

In this chapter:

❖ How kids make friends
❖ Lack of friendship-making skills results in long-term harm
❖ An "ages and stages" outline for friendship making

Chapter 3
A Developmental Approach to Friendship

"Hold a true friend with both hands."
—Nigerian Proverb

BETTER SOCIAL SKILLS mean greater social competence. Social competence creates high self-esteem, which creates more social competence, thus creating higher self-esteem. Greater social competence means greater prosocial behavior, which creates more community. Greater social competence means better social support, which increases social competence. Greater social support means greater intimacy, better health, and better quality of life. These upward feedback loops create ascending spirals of success and effectiveness that improve other social skills also.

Downward spirals can happen, too. For example, children (or adults!) who cannot accept themselves will not be able to accept others. Those with a low self-esteem will be nervous or hostile, rejecting, and unpredictable. They will be meteorically unstable and will put up walls when they feel vulnerable. Their agitated and irrational state sets up an interaction where another person does not know how to respond or give proper encouragement. The person with the low self-image interprets this social ambiguity in a hostile manner, confirming the idea that others are hostile. This interaction becomes a downward cycle. Children with low self-esteem have fewer friends, which makes them more isolated; more isolation makes for fewer friends. Children on the downward cycle try to find acceptance, through means that are usually incompetent and misguided (such as the use of chemicals or membership in gangs).

Friendship-making is not instinctual or genetically known.

Friendship-making is not instinctual or genetically known. Through practice, trial, error, and learning, we grow in our ability to make and understand friends.

Kids Without Friendship-Making Skills

Without friendships, children can have a life that is despairing and unbearable. If friendships are difficult, children may respond by becoming gloppily dependent or angrily bitter. Socially withdrawn or rejected children end up in psychiatric institutions or in jail by a far, far greater percentage than the average population. Research in Minnesota prisons for females found that virtually every prisoner had socially incompetent childhoods—they were not loved and they did not form relationships. In some studies, the number one predictor of adult psychopathology was "being rejected as children."

Yet, despite the crucial importance of social competence, despite the fact that social competence is a better predictor of health and success than IQ, college degrees, or standardized tests, we still allow social skills to develop on their own. We hope that the playground gods will smile on the children, and that social competence will "just kind of happen."

The Ages and Stages of Making Friends

The following is a explanation of how children make friends from birth to age 13 and following. Much of friendship-making revolves around the ability to take another person's point of view.

The ages and stages are a general guide. Not all children fit the chart exactly. Some children go faster than usual, and then slow down, and then speed up again. Some children take longer to move to the new stage, while others go more quickly.

Socially-withdrawn or socially-inept children have a younger friendship age. Sometimes an event like a parental divorce temporarily slows the child down. If you see a child who is "falling behind" according to the chart, it is not proof that the child is growing up to be socially inept. You need to look at the whole picture of the child.

Stage 1: Ages 0-2

The first stage of human friendships is from birth to age two. These children appear to desire company, but they do not play together as much as play in one another's presence.

Children at this age who lag socially won't be helped significantly by more interactions. More likely, simple love and caring would be a better focus of attention.

Stage 2: Ages 2-5

Children in this stage describe friends in concrete characteristics: "Jane is my friend because she lives in a big house," or "he's my friend because he runs fast." Friends are described by their physical or geographic characteristics. Because children focus on visible, concrete characteristics, boys tend to play with boys and girls tend to play with girls.

The primary characteristic of stage 2 is a type of egocentrism. The children at stage 2 still think only of their own needs and *their* side of the relationship. Friendships are generated when a playmate shares candy or gives them a turn. They are not always sure how to respond in social situations. For example, if I see my friend at preschool, I can say "hi" but if I see them at the grocery store, I don't know if I should say "hi" or not.

They are not yet fully concerned about other's needs; they don't yet recognize the give and take of relationships. Children's friendships change as quickly as their needs change. It becomes a full-time job for children to understand who is their friend today, and who is not.

They begin to understand curiosity, and dreaming. They start to understand the varying degrees of emotion such as, "I'm a little mad," or "I'm very, very mad!"

Stage 2 is characterized by creativity, joint fantasy, and shared imagination. Skills and capacities of curiosity, ability to dream, boldness and richness of relationships are generated from the dynamics of this stage. Of course, the rich creativity of this stage is a two-edged sword. While children can express wonderful creativity, they can also really be afraid of the monsters in the closet or the turtleheads under the bed. Children can be victimized by their own imaginations.

Sometimes during this stage, children will try on different personality types. They experiment with behavior that is not "natural" for them. It is normal for children who are experimenting with a role to take it to the extreme—so a child who wants to be assertive might become bossy and even socially aggressive. A child who wants to be a comic might become supersilliously ridiculous. Children will push envelopes to find out where the boundaries are.

Another characteristic of this stage is that children understand relationships enough to begin to develop triangles. "Mom won't let me do this, so I'll go ask my dad." "You can't be Megan's friend if you want to be my friend." The child may try to impress mommy at daddy's expense, or play one parent off the other. The child may put one person off to spend time with another. The child can play out rivalries—not one on one, but in threes. Now the child's play can be the bad guy attacking the helpless doll, but then the doll is rescued by the giant dinosaur. Sometimes imaginary friends are used to fill roles in triangles.

While the child's triangles might be annoying for care-givers, it is a necessary part of development as children learn to understand the complexity of social relationships.

Sometimes, when children are playing together, and another child comes in and wants to play, the response is "You can't play with us, we're already playing." This looks like a snub of the latecomer. However, it frequently isn't an act of cruelty as much as an inability to understand how the latecomer can join. They can't figure out how to incorporate another person into the play they already have going.

Stage 3: Ages 6-12

In stage 3, a give-and-take emerges—this is called *reciprocity*. There is a certain tit-for-tat-ness, a "you take a turn and then I'll take a turn" mentality. Children move from a concern about their own needs into a more reciprocal relationship. There is still, however, a definition of give-and-take that weighs heavily in favor of their own needs. In other words, the child at this age cries out "it's not fair," but fairness is defined by "getting their own way." As the child moves through stage 3, they define reciprocity in a less and less egocentric manner. Eventually, towards stage 4, it becomes an honest mutual collaboration.

The definition of "friends" is now "kids I play with." Friendship is determined by joint activities and concrete, practical experiences.

There is still a possessiveness about relationships. A best friend with Lisa cannot also be best friends with Stacey.

In stage 2, children were defined by their family relationships. In stage 3, children move toward defining themselves based on their peers. Children identify their own place in the playground pecking order. They become experts in identifying who is the coolest, who runs the fastest, etc. The children are attentive to who plays with who and why.

Relations with peers are critical during this stage because it is with peers that children learn the give and take of relationships. While adults will always be critical in children's development, children need other children to practice the giving and taking. Children probably won't learn about the reciprocal nature of friendships from adults, because adults, by nature, are in a power position.

As the children move through this stage, they begin to understand a self-perception apart from social status, and begin to define themselves based on internal ideas. "I like myself because I am good at building with Legos." "I have lots of friends because I play well with lots of different kids."

Warning Signs At This Stage:

- **Children who are frequently rebuffed.** All children get rebuffed, but a consistent message of rejection over the years can lead to social problems.
- **Hoverers.** Children who don't know how to join in with the others. They exhibit an uncertainty about relationships, so they hover outside the group. They hope someone will invite them to play, but they don't know how to initiate their own joining. When they finally burst in, the others have already moved on.

- **Loners.** Some kids are quieter than others, but a persistent pattern of *never* entering a relationship can be problematic. Social withdrawal is a red flag that should tell caregivers that the child is experiencing some stalling on the road of development.
- **Bullies.** Left unchecked, bullying can grow into serious abuse. Bullies tend to be people who have been hurt, and so they desire to hurt others so that no one can find acceptance. The maxim is true, "hurt people hurt people."
- **Manipulators.** Every child, at one time or another, tries to manipulate others into doing their bidding. However, a constant pattern over the long term suggests that the child is stuck in their ability to understand that give-and-take.

Stage 4: Ages 13 and following

Stage 4 begins with a recognition that friends have rights, even when they are not meeting one's own needs. They realize that one friend cannot fill all their needs—and even if a friend *could* fill all their needs, that is not even necessarily desirable. Friendship becomes a mutual sharing of intimacy, secrets, and is based on trust and acceptance of each other.

Self-esteem becomes more stable. The young adolescent is no longer tossed to and fro by every compliment or caustic quip. Teenagers can control, to a greater degree than before, what happens to their self-esteem when someone says something negative about them. This comes at a time, paradoxically, when they become hyper-attentive to what others think about them.

Kids at this stage develop some early moral thinking. They can begin to think ethically—how "this isn't right" and "that is wrong." They can believe that something's not fair even if it is against their own desires.

Figure #4: Stages of Friendship-Making

Stage 2: Ages 2-5

- Focus on concrete characteristics
- Think about their side of the relationship
- Don't fully recognize other's needs
- Value creativity and joint fantasy
- Try on different personalities
- Begin to understand triangles

Stage 3: Ages 6-12

- Reciprocity emerges
- Continue to think more about own needs, despite rhetoric of fairness
- Friends are "kids I play with"
- Become possessive about friendships
- Begin to use self-perception and self-reflection

Stage 4: Ages 13 and older

- Allow friends to have their own rights
- Can suspend their own desires for others
- Consider friendship a sharing of intimacy and trust
- Can evaluate other's opinions
- Show a development of moral thinking—what's right and wrong

Here's the Point

Social development follows the same patterns as the other perspectives of development. Knowing social development and the deepening patterns of friendship can help those who work with children in their tasks of guidance and the learning of social skills.

Frequently Asked Questions

Q Should I make kids play together who are playing alone?

A The first question to ask yourself is why you want them to play together. Is that your need to have the kids playing together?

Some kids like to play alone. They might have spent all day in school with other kids, at home they have to play with their siblings, and they never have a chance to play by themselves. "Playing by oneself" is not a warning sign.

The warning sign is when a child *never* plays with anyone else and shows no desire to *ever* play with anyone else. Remember, warning signs are only warning signs when there is a *pattern* of that behavior over the *long term*.

Q What do I do with kids who intentionally, with malice and forethought, exclude someone else from playing with them?

A First, you should ask, "was it really out of malice?" Younger children often exclude others, not because they want to hurt someone, but simply that once they get started on an activity, they can't figure out how to incorporate another person. Psychologists call this an "irreversibility of thought." You could bring it to their attention, or suggest ways that the other friend might play.

If it was an intentional act of insult and hurt, then, of course, you have a different issue. Then, you have to find out from them why they thought it was okay to behave that way. You'll have to remind them that "that kind of behavior is not tolerated here." You'll need to hold them accountable in the same way that you hold a child accountable who hits another child.

Discussion Questions

1. Give some examples, from children you know, of the characteristics of each stage.
2. What is the difference between developmentally appropriate and socially acceptable? What do you do when these two areas clash?
3. What should a professional do when they see the warning signs for poor relationship building?
4. What kind of activities would promote positive friendship skills for each age and stage?

Helpful Readings

Greenspan, S. (1994). *Playground politics: Understanding the emotional life of your school-age child.* Reading, MA: Addison-Wesley Publishing Co.

Kostelnick, M. (2001). *Guiding Children's Social Development, Fourth Edition.* Delmar Publishers.

Reference Notes

Information on the criminal justice system comes from:
*   M. Ryan, personal communication regarding Minnesota prisons, and Howells, K. (1981). Social relationships in violent offenders. In S.S. Duck and R. Gilmour (eds.). *Personal Relationships 3: Personal Relationships in Disorder.* London: Academic Press.

Important historical works in the field of developmental psychology are:
*   Beard, R. (1969). *An outline of Piaget's developmental psychology.* New York: Mentor Books.
*   Elkind, D. (1994). *Understanding your child: Birth to sixteen.* Needham Heights, MA: Allyn and Bacon.
*   Elkind, D. (1988). *The hurried child.* Needham Heights, MA: Allyn and Bacon.
*   Erikson, E. (1963). *Childhood and society.* New York: W.W. Norton and Company.

- Freud, S. (1937/1957). *A general selection from the works of Sigmund Freud.* New York: Doubleday and Company.
- Kegan, R. (1982). *The evolving self.* Cambridge, MA: Harvard University Press.
- Kohlberg, L. (1984). *Morality, moral behavior, and moral development.* New York: John Wiley and Sons.
- Selman, R.L., & Selman, A.P. (October, 1979). Children's ideas about friendship: A new theory. *Psychology Today*, 13, pp. 71-114.

SOCIAL SKILL CLUSTERS

Social Skill Clusters

In this chapter:

❖ Confidence is believing that you are a capable person
❖ Children express confidence in various ways
❖ Adults can help create an environment in which children feel valued

Chapter 4
Confidence:
I Can Do It

"So every time you stumble, Never grumble.
Next time you'll bumble even less.
For up from the ashes, up from the ashes,
grow the roses of success."
> —The Imprisoned Scientists, "The Roses of
> Success," *Chitty Chitty Bang Bang*

RANDY BOASTS CONSTANTLY about his
own accomplishments. Sometimes he remembers
events selectively, so that he can brag about
his prowess even more. Randy is
insecure, with a low self-esteem
that is hidden by a facade of self-
aggrandizement.

Sally can laugh at herself, and
joke with others. She tries new things
even when she knows there is a good
chance of failure. She seems to have
an accurate picture of her strengths,
weaknesses, abilities, and limitations.

Confidence is the willingness to try new things, because failure is simply another opportunity to learn.

Confidence is believing that you are a capable
person. It's having an accurate picture of who
you are and what you can do. Confidence is the
willingness to try new things, because failure is
simply another opportunity to learn.

Confidence is related to optimism. Martin Seligman makes a convincing case for the character of optimism as the primary protective factor for depression and low functioning. Optimism is the belief that while bad events may be a setback, they do not hamstring your success for the long term. Pessimism on the other hand, is the belief that bad events will continue to hamstring your success.

Confidence consists of two main components. The first component is that I am *doing well*. This is the inner belief that I am competent and capable. The second component is *feeling good*. This is the feeling that I am loved and that I belong.

Figure #5: A Self-Assessment of Confidence

1. I have an accurate picture of myself.
2. I can identify things I am good at, as well as things I do poorly.
3. I know that I am valuable, regardless what others think.
4. I have significance. I am worthwhile.
5. I am generally optimistic about the future.
6. I know that I am acceptable even if my behavior does not measure up.
7. I have the skills and knowledge to contribute to the group.
8. I know that my failures don't define me as a person or dictate my worth.

Children with Confidence

As children grow in their confidence they will set higher standards, strive to achieve new levels of success, and take reasonable risks.

Children with confidence show a healthy attitude of play. A nine-year-old girl grabs a pogo stick and starts hopping around. She hops down the driveway, across the street and up her friend's driveway without ever putting her foot down. When asked how she got to be so good at pogo hopping she replies, "Well, first Danielle and I tried to get ten hops, then once we could do that we kept raising the number. I think the highest we ever counted was 300. Now we don't count anymore, we just hop."

When children have developed a healthy sense of confidence:

- **They will be independent thinkers**
  They will not feel like they *have to* follow the group. They can choose to follow the group, or choose not to. Children with confidence will articulate their own thoughts—thoughts that they didn't hear on TV.
- **They will be able to make plans**
  They'll have some sense of the future. Statements like, "I want to be a fire fighter" or "I'm going to be a tennis star" show a sign of making plans.
- **They will be able to contribute**
  Children with confidence believe they have worthwhile things to offer a group discussion. That doesn't mean they dominate the group discussion—they can listen to others' contributions as well. Children who dominate

the discussion may well have low confidence, as they are threatened by the lack of control and those who have ideas different than their own.

- **They will engage in discovery**
  Children with confidence will try new things. They will get a thrill out of the newness of a challenge, and not be as concerned if they succeed or fail.

- **They will see themselves as worthwhile**
  Overall, confident children will believe they are worthwhile, that they are cared for and they are significant.

- **They will practice self-awareness**
  Confident children are able to see cues in their environment. They walk into a new environment and know how to behave. Further, they'll have a realistic perception of themselves. They'll know what they are good at, and what they are not good at—and they'll know that their value as a person isn't based on which skills they have or don't have.

Some Warning Signs

There is no single warning sign that is evidence of a lack of confidence. And all children (and adults!) go through temporary periods of low confidence. However, a *pattern* of the following warning signs over the *long term*, may be a cause for more individualized attention from the care-giving adults.

- **They're afraid to try new things**
  They don't like to try new things. They
  frequently say, "I can't do that." The problem
  for a child with low confidence is that they
  feel like they don't have the choice to gamble
  with the possibility of failure. Like having too
  few chips in a poker game, they can't commit
  all they have and then lose. These children
  will have lots of excuses—"that's stupid,"
  "that's boring," etc.
- **Remembering selectively**
  All children—and adults—remember
  selectively. We have to remember selectively
  because we can't keep every detail of every
  interaction in our head, so we only remember
  the important things. All children will
  remember the stuff that protects their self-
  image. However, children with low confidence
  have an *inability* to remember completely.
  They might remember the things that make
  them appear more competent—and they'll
  blame others for their failures. Or, they'll
  remember only the things that remind them
  that they are failures—also a sign of low
  confidence.
- **Following the crowd or being a loner**
  Either extreme can be a warning sign.
  Children with low confidence will not
  have the emotional strength to say "no" to
  negative peer pressure. They follow the crowd
  because they lack the ability to go against
  the group. Or, in a different manifestation
  of low confidence, they will avoid all people,
  becoming a loner.

Self-Reflection as a Tool for Confidence

As children grow up, a healthy sense of confidence will provide a foundation for resiliency and self-reflection. They'll grow up with the ability to understand their own actions, which is the source of self-understanding, personal growth, and learning.

As children grow up, a healthy sense of confidence will provide a foundation for resiliency and self-reflection.

One of the problems in human development is that we tend to only hear information that agrees with what we already believe. We tend to fit what we see around what we already believe, and fail to notice the information that doesn't match our preconceptions. So, if children become convinced that they are incompetent, it becomes difficult to change that self-assessment. It is difficult because children who feel incompetent will immediately discount any information that suggests they are competent. We need to reach children early and often with the message that they are worthwhile and significant. And when children already feel undervalued, they need consistent messages of value; when those messages are consistent, they may begin to reflect on that and think it through—this is the process of self-reflection. It is through self-reflection that people can change.

Case Study #2: Tim and Sophie

Tim and Sophie are in the same class at school. Most of the class plays dodgeball at recess. When Tim gets hit with the ball, he blames a teammate for obscuring his vision. Sometimes, he'll limp off the playground, pretending that he hurt his ankle. Sophie gets hit with the ball, too, but just giggles at her misfortune. When they retell the dodgeball stories, Tim and Sophie seem to remember it differently. Tim always seems to remember that he was the last one standing.

Tim gets mad when the plans for recess change. If he was expecting dodgeball, he gets mad when he has to change. Sophie seems to go with the flow better. Sometimes she has an idea, and sometimes she agrees to what another child wants to do. Tim likes dodgeball, and plays it well, but refuses to play a new game that he hasn't played before. Sophie likes to try the new games, even when she can't do well.

Tim always seems a little worried when recess starts—and perhaps a little preoccupied with what will happen at recess. Sophie is just glad to be outside.

How Adults Can Help

- **Show unconditional acceptance.**
  Help children understand that you like them and they are valuable, no matter what. Greet every child warmly. It can make an enormous difference if children believe that you are honestly happy to see them. Even when children misbehave, we can avoid the "shame on you" mentality. We can calmly state, "I'm sorry you made that choice, but here are the consequences of that choice." Correcting

misbehavior can be shaming, or it can be educative; strive to make it educative. Don't let yesterday's misbehaviors influence your interactions with children today.

- **Celebrate with children.**
  Help children feel like you're with them when they succeed. Even if it's as simple as "You scored higher than ever on our video game!" Children will feel significant and worthwhile when they believe you honestly care about their successes, however small. Further, you can let them celebrate your successes, too. They will feel valued to be included in your celebrations.

- **Support them in their failures.**
  Perhaps even more important than celebrating their successes is to be with them in their failures. Children who fail will often wonder if people will still like them. Adults need to show children that failure has nothing to do with how much we like them. And when children fail, we don't need to "say the right thing" or "counsel them appropriately." We just need to be *with them*. When we don't connect failure with competency, then children can see more easily that failures are opportunities for growth and learning.

- **Avoid conditional statements**
  Statements like, "I like you because…" should be avoided. Anything that attaches *our sentiment* to *their behavior* can feed their belief that "I have to earn others' love." We can say, "I appreciate when you clean up when you're done," but don't attach "I like you" to anything else.

- **Teach children how to reflect on the events in their life.**
  Self-awareness is a critical part of confidence. When children and youth can think about their behavior ("Why did I get so angry?" "Why don't I want to play with Susie?" "Why am I uncomfortable around Sydney?"). Children who are reflective are much more apt to be confident in who they are.

Here's the Point

Children with confidence develop a foundation for living. Independence, feeling worthwhile and capable, and a desire to learn are results of being confident. Adults can help children with this set of skills when they provide unconditional acceptance.

✔ Try This

One way to teach confidence is to help children learn to recognize when they and other people do a good job. We use compliments to recognize a job well done. Confidence has fertile soil in a culture that makes compliments a habit. It's easy to find children skilled at insults, but they often show less expertise at compliments. Ask children to mention good things that they have seen, heard, or felt. If children have a difficult time understanding the idea of compliments, a "Compliment Hunter" bulletin board can collect examples.

Frequently Asked Questions

Q What's the difference between self-esteem, self-concept, and confidence?

A Self-*concept* is the picture we have of ourselves. Self-*esteem* is how we *feel* about that picture of ourselves. *Confidence*, as we use it here, is an umbrella term for all the skills and perceptions that reveal what we believe about ourselves.

Q What's the difference between confidence and over-confidence?

A A healthy sense of confidence is to believe that you are significant and worthwhile. Over-confidence, as the term is usually used, means "a belief in your own abilities that exceed reality." In fact, as we use the term here, "a belief in your own abilities that exceed reality" actually represents *low* confidence. Typically, this kind of over-confidence is a façade that protects children from facing the fact that they can't do something.

Discussion Questions

1. As you grew up, which adults helped you with the skills of confidence? Who were they and what actions impacted you?
2. Are there children at your site that exhibit long-term, multiple warning signs? What is their behavior like? What things do they say that suggest to you that they have low confidence?

3. Describe a child at your site that has high confidence.
4. Describe adults who have low confidence. What attitudes, behavior, or conversations might they exhibit that would reveal low confidence?
5. In what ways have you seen adult sentiment connected with children's behavior ("I like you because...")?
6. Discuss the case study of Tim and Sophie. What actions give you clues to their level of confidence? What might you prescribe for them?
7. What are some other ways to help children with confidence?

Helpful Readings

Seligman, M. (1996). *The optimistic child: A revolutionary program that safeguards children against depression and builds lifelong resilience.* New York: Perennial Press.

Seligman, M. (1998). *Learned optimism: How to change your mind and life.* New York: Free Press.

In this chapter:

❖ *Locus of control* is when I take responsibility for what I do
❖ Adults can help children learn to take responsibility for their actions

Chapter 5
Control: I Am Responsible for My Actions

"Believe that life is worth living and your belief will help create the fact."
—William James, 1842-1910

"RYAN STOLE my pencil! I *had* to hit him!" pleads Stevie, looking as if a great injustice is about to be thrust upon him. For Stevie, the assault was Ryan's own fault. "If Ryan hadn't stole my pencil, he wouldn't have gotten hit!"

Control, as a social skill set, refers to taking control over your own behavior. It means to take responsibility for your actions and behavior. Stevie is not taking responsibility for his own actions.

A term used in the social scientific literature is *locus of control*, and it has to do with "how we take responsibility for our actions." An *external* locus of control means that we believe our behavior is someone else's responsibility. An *internal* locus of control means that we understand that we are in charge of our own behavior.

A person with an external locus of control believes in good luck and bad luck. "You can't really control what happens to you, so you just hope for the best." A person with an internal locus of control will say, "My choices matter. I can't always control what happens to me, but I can control how I respond to what happens to me." A person with an internal locus of control believes that decisions and choices have a powerful effect on their future.

A person with an external locus of control might say things like this:	A person with an internal locus of control might say things like this:
Ryan made me hit him.	I felt angry and then made a choice to hit Ryan.
The bus left without me.	I didn't organize my time well enough to be at the place where the bus said it would be.
They stopped delivering the newspaper to my house.	I didn't make the payments on time, so the newspaper stopped giving me the paper.
The keys are lost.	I can't remember where I put my keys.
All the other kids are doing it.	No matter how many kids are doing it, I still must decide if I should do it.

People without the skill of control believe that nothing they do has much to do with their future. What happens is simply luck, fate, and the roll of the dice. If the Success Gods smile on us, we succeed in life. If they frown, we crash and burn.

The skill of control is about self-discipline and taking responsibility for our own choices. It means to be responsible and self-controlled. It is to understand that we have choices to make, and those choices impact our future.

Figure #6: A Self-Assessment of Control

1. I—rather than others—am in control of my life.
2. No one forces me to do anything. I choose what I do.
3. I'm responsible for my own behavior.
4. My choices and decisions have an impact on my future.
5. I don't give up easily.
6. My life is not a series of random events—it's a pattern based on the choices I've made.
7. Typically, success is due to hard work, rather than chance or luck.

Children with Control

Children begin their lives with an external locus of control. Kids younger than first grade will consistently show an external locus of control, and this is normal and natural. Signs of a maturing internal locus will start showing up in first and second grade. Signs of the internal locus of control will be occasional and spotty, but—hopefully—will occur with greater and greater frequency as the child grows toward adolescence.

These elementary years are the prime time for children to learn control. Children can learn that they indeed are responsible for their own choices and actions. However, learning the skill of control only happens when the adults in the lives of children help them to gain a perspective on social situations. Adults can help children realize that they are indeed responsible for their own behavior.

Interestingly, children will use a variety of techniques to absolve themselves of control. They will argue that it isn't their fault. They will "forget" the rule, hoping that the adult will take over. When inattentive adults take over for children, it reinforces their view that "I'm not responsible for my actions."

Control: I Am Responsible For My Actions

One of the ways children learn responsibility is to *have responsibility*. Then, too, they must suffer the consequences of their failure to comply. It is important to give children responsibility, but also to not rescue them too quickly.

For example, if we force children to do their homework in a school-age program, are they learning responsibility? Or are we teaching children that adults are going to take over the responsibility of what their schedule should be? While forcing children to do their homework may get their homework completed, it does not help support their skill of responsibility.

When children have developed a healthy sense of control:

- **They can think beyond their first response**
  Children with this social skill are better at controlling their impulses. They might want to do something, but continue to think about it and come to a wiser choice. Children with control are no longer *ruled* by their impulses; rather, they *have* impulses that they can control.

- **They develop an ability to choose their response**
  Lots of things happen to people, but we always have the ability to choose our response. Children with control have a much larger repertoire of responses. Children without control have few responses—and those responses are usually based in aggression or fear.

- **They are better at managing their own behavior**
  Children with control don't behave because an adult is watching. They behave better than children without control because they can manage their own behavior. They accept more responsibility, they display more patience, they are able to be more attentive and stay on task. They do not manage their behavior based only on the fear of the adult caregivers.
- **They don't see themselves as helpless victims of an overbearing world**
  When children develop an internal locus of control, they are able to view themselves as in control of their response to life and can make plans for their future. Such children do not see themselves powerless against the future. They do not see themselves as victims. They are able to take responsibility for their actions.
- **They will be able to delay gratification**
  They can see a toy they want, for example, and know that they can get it another time. They can put off their desire to have something *right now*, and understand that waiting is okay. They know the difference between wants and needs.

Some Warning Signs

All children exhibit times of external locus of control, especially younger children. As children grow older, the skill of control manifests itself in growing and more frequent signs of self-management and responsibility. So, warning signs are problems only if the signs are persistent and chronic.

- **Consistent blaming of others**
  A warning sign would be children who constantly blame other children for their behavior. The child who says, "Shelly made me do it" is normal. The child who *constantly* says that about *every* aspect of behavior, who constantly complains that "it's not my fault" could be revealing a low control level.

- **Persistently victimized**
  "Being helpless against the world" is the feeling worn by people with low control. Since children with an external locus of control feel as if they have no influence on the events around them, they often find themselves in situations where they are bullied and intimidated.

- **Self-management only when adults are watching**
  Children with low control behave when adults are present, but immediately misbehave when adults leave the room. In fact, "self-management only when adults are watching" is not really self-management at all… it's simply the avoidance of punishment.

- **Engage in goal-destructive behavior**
  "Goal-destructive" means that people act in

ways that are contrary to their stated goals. So, for example, they may say they want to be on the football team, but they don't show up for practice. Then, when they get kicked off the team, they say, "that coach wouldn't let me on the team—he was out to get me."

Control Skills: Looking to the Future

As children grow into adolescents and adults, they need the internal locus of control for a stability of life. Adolescents without the skill of control will drink and drive, and then they will be angry at the police for catching them. Young adults will use illicit chemicals, because they don't see a connection between the mind-wasting drugs and their future. Adults with an external locus of control will be enraged at the airline flight attendant when the airplane is late (and then the judge will mandate anger management classes, which won't work because the problem is not about anger, it's about how that person sees the world).

Children who grow up with high control skills tend to have a stability in life...

People without control always want someone else to solve their problems, because they believe those problems—and the solution—are beyond their control.

On the other hand, children who grow up with high control skills tend to have a stability in life that evades their poor-control peers. They take responsibility for their choices, their health, and their behavior. However, they won't take responsibility for choices or events that are truly beyond their control.

Case Study #3: Stevie, Ms. Sponge, and Ms. Roper

The following is a conversation between a school-age care provider and Stevie, a third grader. Some commentary is given in the right column.

Interaction	Commentary on the interaction
Ms. Sponge: Stevie, why did you hit Ryan?	
Stevie: He stole my pencil, I had to hit him!	Here is the evidence of his external locus of control.
Ms. Sponge: What is the rule about hitting?	She misses the opportunity to challenge his locus.
Stevie: I don't know.	This is Stevie's way of getting Ms. Sponge to take over.
Ms Sponge: The rule is to keep your hands to yourself, and no hitting.	She doesn't see his technique, so she takes over.
Stevie remains silent.	Stevie, still believing the assault was not his fault, waits for his "unjust punishment."
Ms Sponge: What's the consequence when you hit someone here?	
Stevie: I don't know.	Again, Stevie attempts to get Ms. Sponge to take over.
Ms. Sponge: Well, I'll tell you. I'm going to call your parents and they'll have to pick you up.	She does. This reinforces Stevie's view that "what happens to me is up to other people."

	Here's another way it could have happened, with a more attentive care-giver:
Ms. Roper: Stevie, why did you hit Ryan?	
Stevie: He stole my pencil, I had to hit him!	Here is the evidence of his external locus of control.
Ms. Roper: You mean, he stole your pencil so you chose to hit him?	She challenges his perspective.
Stevie: I guess.	
Ms. Roper: What is the rule about hitting?	
Stevie: I don't know.	This is Stevie's way of getting Ms. Roper to take over.
Ms Roper: Okay, well, why don't you sit right here until you remember what the rule is.	She doesn't get drawn in to his trap. She makes it his responsibility.
(She gets up and starts to leave)	
Stevie: Oh, I remember. You're supposed to keep your hands to yourself and not hit others.	Stevie magically remembers what the rule is.
Ms Roper: And what's the consequence when you hit someone here?	
Stevie: I don't know.	Again, Stevie attempts to get Ms. Roper to take over.
Ms. Roper: Okay, well, why don't you sit right here until you remember.	She doesn't get drawn in to his trap. She makes it his responsibility.
Stevie: Oh, I remember. We have to call my parents and I have to go home.	
Ms. Roper: That's right. I'm sorry you made the choice to hit Ryan. But now, you'll have to live with the consequences of your choices.	She reinforces his responsibility one more time.

How Adults Can Help

An attentive care-giver can help children develop their control skills. No single adult, nor single interaction, can impart the skills of control. But many adults, over the course of many interactions, will help the child learn the skills needed for life.

- **Observe children carefully.**
  Careful observation of the child, and what they say, will give you a sense of the child's skill level. The ability to observe children and youth is critical to guiding the use of control skills.

- **Give children strategies to control their own behavior.**
  Discuss with children the importance of self-management, and ask them how you can partner with them to control their behavior. You might say something like, "How about if I whisper 'stop and think' when it looks like you might lose control? Would that help?" Perhaps a reminder like "practice your patience" or even a non-verbal cue will help the child remember to get control of themselves. For children with low control skill, this can be a powerful reminder that self-management is important and it is their responsibility, not the adult's.

- **Help children understand that they can't control others.**
  When children say, "but Ryan made me mad!" you can be sympathetic with their emotion but try to correct the perspective. "I understand that you're upset... but Ryan took your pencil,

and that made you mad, so you *chose* to hit him." Children (and adults!) without the skill of control spend a lot of time trying to get others to do what they want them to do. The skill of control is to realize that you can't control others, but you can control your own reaction to others.

- **Allow natural consequences to occur when it is safe to do so.**
  Natural consequences are a part of life. If adults rescue children during their entire childhood, then the children will grow up without an ability to see or understand consequences.

Here's the Point

The social skill of control will enable children to engage in self-management. They will be better able to take responsibility for themselves and make appropriate positive choices.

Frequently Asked Questions

Q You say we should give children responsibility, but then not rescue them. Doesn't that set them up for failure?

A It's true that you never want to set kids up for failure. So, if you know they are going to fail at a task, then they shouldn't be given the responsibility for the task. Usually, they need to be taught more knowledge or have better skills before they are given the task. But, if they have the knowledge or skills to do a task, and they start to fail, if we leap in and rescue them, they won't get learn that their decisions matter... they'll always wait for someone to rescue them.

Q How do you hold kids accountable for their actions?

A "Holding people accountable" is not about catching kids when they're misbehaving, it's about making sure they use the skills that we know they have. We can't hold kids accountable for skills they haven't learned. So, we must understand "accountability" within the context of the children and what their skills are. Accountability is not about catching and punishing misbehavior, it's about our belief in the child.

When an Olympic athlete is about to take the field, they'll give a glance at their coach. The coach will give a smile and a nod, nonverbally saying, "You can do it. I believe in you." That's what holding kids accountable means. It's a way to remind them of the social skills kids know, and being able to use those skills in new situations.

Discussion Questions

1. In your own life, when did you start realizing that you had control over your choices and actions?
2. Talk about some common situations at your site. What will children with low control skills say or do? What will children with high control skills say or do?

3. What are some ways that adults take away children's control?
4. What are some reasons why adults might rescue children?
5. Which societal trends or attitudes reinforce an external locus of control? Which ones reinforce an internal locus?

Helpful Readings

McGraw, P. (2001). *Self matters: Creating your life from the inside out.* New York: Simon and Schuster.

Reference Notes

The concept of "locus of control" was developed by Julian Rotter and first published in 1966. The construct has been found to have very significant validity and reliability.

In this chapter:

❖ The skill of coping is needed when things don't go our way
❖ Children may not always understand what is going on in their body
❖ Adult caregivers can find ways for children to relax and de-stress

Chapter 6
Coping: I Can Manage the Hard Times

"Make yourself necessary to somebody. Do not make life hard to any."
—Ralph Waldo Emerson, 1803-1882

BRIAN HAS HEADACHES. Xia's stomach hurts. Charlie itches constantly. Renee gets hives. Perhaps 25% of children have some physical symptom that has a social or psychological cause.

Saundra pulls her hair. Tommy is wild and out of control. Diana has mood extremes. Aquanetta hides her emotional pain by making others mad at her. Karen hides her inside pain by hurting herself on the outside. Gregory has a panic attack every time adults move quickly toward him. These behavioral issues can also have social or psychological causes.

Coping is the ability to "handle it" when things are going poorly. If the stress is too much to do, grief from a death in the family, or anxiety from incessant teasing, children need ways to cope. When things don't go as we want them to or need them to, we need the

> **Coping is the ability to "handle it" when things are going poorly.**

skills to manage the stress, fear, grief, or anxiety. We need the skill of coping.

Coping, like the other social skills in this book, is an umbrella term. *Coping* includes such skills as:

- Knowing how to relax
- Not sweating the small stuff
- Knowing when we need help from an adult
- Being able to go with the flow
- Handling frustration and annoyance in a positive manner
- Being able to laugh at oneself
- Being angry without being violent or inappropriate

Figure #7: A Self-Assessment of Coping

1. I can go with the flow when plans change.
2. Generally, I'm pretty self-reliant.
3. I can usually find the resources I need to do what I need to do.
4. I know how to relax when I need to.
5. I can read my own body signs when stress becomes too high.
6. I have people I can talk to when I need it.
7. I don't fly off the handle.
8. I don't lose my sense of humor in a crisis.
9. I know the difference between things that I have control over and things that I don't.

Children with Coping

Coping, like all social skills, is a learned behavior. It is a plethora of skills, attitudes, and knowledge, including health, nutrition, exercise, play, rest, social support, and the ability to de-stress. It is the ability to deal with life stress while keeping a positive outlook.

The skills of this cluster assist school-age children as they learn they cannot control life. School-age children learn that they cannot control their friends, they cannot control the likes and dislikes of their peers, and they cannot control the world around them. All they can do is choose *how* to respond to that lack of control.

Children who are learning to cope will:

- Talk about the resources they have.
- Understand that they are stressed, but that they will not *always* feel this way.
- Work to analyze social situations.
- Start to understand how to not put themselves in positions where they could be victimized.
- Ask questions.
- Know adults in whom they can confide.

Coping skills are clearly demonstrated when a child is able to make objective, conscious decisions. When they do this, they clearly illustrate that they are capable of making and applying purposeful decisions, and are no longer relying on instinctual, knee-jerk reactions. Whenever there is a delay between the incident and the response, the chances are greater that the reaction will be positive and appropriate.

Coping: I Can Manage the Hard Times

Some Warning Signs

Not all coping skills are positive and beneficial. Unfortunately, many coping skills that are frequently employed by both children *and* adults are dysfunctional. We may shout at others, get violent, withdraw, or even get physically sick. We often withdraw and push away from the very people who could help us. It is not uncommon for both children and adults to use dysfunctional coping mechanism which actually hinder real coping.

The following are some of the warning signs that may help adults see when a child is not learning the skill of coping. Remember—no single symptom or event shows a lack of coping skill. It's the pattern of behaviors that are important.

- **Abdominal pain, headaches, or other physical symptoms**
  The most common physical symptom is probably abdominal pain; it may affect 10-15% of children. Other physical symptoms might be headaches or insomnia. Obviously, these may also be caused by medical problems, so a physician should make that determination. However, if the child is undergoing some kind of stress, then "abdominal pain" could be a piece of the overall picture.

- **Reactions not commensurate with events**
  When the adult facilitator suggests that everyone go outside for a game, Sally screams at the top of her lungs. This is a reaction not

commensurate with the schedule change. This suggests that something else is going on with Sally.

- **Emotional changes that are not typical of the child**
  Stu used to be gentle and kind, but now he is surly and short-tempered. Tony used to be happy and fun, but now he is sad all the time. Jennifer used to be gregarious and extraverted, but now she is a loner. When drastic changes occur in children's emotional makeup, there may be some coping issues going on.

- **Lack of humor**
  Children should laugh and play. It is the nature of childhood. When they constantly appear solemn and serious, it could suggest a problem. Of course, every child is sad sometimes, but when the sadness is chronic, something else could be going on in the child's life.

> *Children should laugh and play. It is the nature of childhood.*

Coping as a Rare Skill?

Of the seven social skills in this book, coping might be the skill fewest people have. Too many adults have never learned good coping skills, so they rely on instincts, knee-jerk reactions, or other dysfunctional strategies.

However, when children learn this important skill, they will be better at problem solving, more able to accept events, better at follow-through, and will be more determined to seek the resources to resolve an issue.

Coping: I Can Manage the Hard Times

Children's statements about themselves not only reflect what they're thinking, but the statements can actually *affect* their physical feelings of anxiety. When children say positive, affirming statements to themselves and about themselves, they often have less anxiety and feel more capable of handling stressful moments. For example, a child who is able to say statements such as, "I am brave and smart and can take good care of myself" is typically able to cope better than the child who continually says things like, "I can't handle this, "My stuff is always bad," or Mine isn't good enough." Adults can get insight into the skills of children through careful observation.

✔ Try This!

"What do you do when…" is a coping skill game. It can be done anytime, anywhere. Start off with the phrase, "What do you do when you're _____?" Fill in the blank with simple things first, like *hungry* and *tired*. Then fill in the blank with more complex ideas like *sad, hurt, angry*, or *confused*. The answers that children give could reveal areas where teaching is needed, but more often children share great ideas to cope.

Case Study #4: Brock, Jake, and Jordan

Brock, Jake, and Jordan sat down to play a board game. Brock was a kindergartener and couldn't read. Jake (a second grader) and Jordan (a fourth grader) were brothers. The board game requires the players to read a card for special movements they can do during their turn. When the game started, the boys decided to take turns by simply saying, "I go first." "Me second." They weren't sitting in order around the game board. As play progressed, the turns kept getting mixed up, which usually resulted in a mild disagreement. In addition, Brock couldn't read the cards, so his turn took longer. The other boys tried to help Brock read the cards, but they usually disagreed about what the card actually meant. After a few minutes, their voices got louder, brows more furrowed, and patience became quite short. The program supervisor had been watching this take place. He had been teaching about coping skills during the morning group time. The previous week he had taught about self-control. With a calm, non-anxious presence, he came to the board game participants and complimented them on using good self-control by not letting their fight get out of hand. Then, he coached them to try using some coping skills. The boys took a deep breath, counted to ten like they had practiced, and laughed because they used funny voices on 8, 9, and 10. The supervisor mentioned that it looked like they were having trouble taking turns and reading the cards. Spontaneously, one of the boys asked a fifth grader to play with them and help read the cards. The other child joined, and suggested that they take turns around the table.

How Adults Can Help

Here are a few ways the adult care-giver can help:

- **Be calm. Life is not a crisis.**
  You can be an example of good coping skills. When you can't use this room, when schedules change, when things don't happen like you planned, you can show children a calm response. In the grand scheme of things, ten years from now, no one will remember the schedule change that happened today. Enjoy the journey.

- **Help children read their own body signals.**
  Children are not always good at understanding their own body. They are not good at interpreting the signals sent by their body. Perhaps they don't know why they breathe fast, or why their stomach hurts, or their head hurts, or why they itch all the time. They may not understand that when they have a hyped-up, anxious feeling inside, that a few quiet, deep breaths will often help.

- **Know when to refer children to get more help.**
  The best course of action is typically *not* to tell the parents that their kid needs psychological help (unless you've been trained in pediatric psychopathology). But if you see patterns of behavior that concern you, talk with parents, other staff, their classroom teachers, or whoever will give insight. If you find that there is general concern, you can go to the parents and say something like, "We're seeing some recent behaviors in Julie that concern us,

and here's why." Typically, the parents know their child better than you, so it becomes their decision to seek professional help for the child.

- **Know when to allow children to let off steam.**
  When kids need to let off some steam, they should be allowed to do something active or fun. Help them know that it's okay to take a break and play a game. It's okay to play something wild when the stress inside them is building. Help kids read their own needs, and then channel that into something useful, fun, and positive.

Here's the Point

We all benefit when children develop an internal ability to view life's ups and downs with a positive outlook. When children see themselves as their own best resource they will have an assurance that they can overcome any situation.

✔ Try This!

Some "letting off steam" things to do:
- Run outside
- Talk to someone
- Sing songs
- Draw a picture
- Play a game
- Relax each part of your body, one part at a time
- Find some crayons and a coloring book
- Write a letter to yourself
- Read a book that you don't *have* to read
- Sculpt with clay

Frequently Asked Questions

Q How do you help kids who seem to panic really easily?

A First, determine whether it's panic, or a way to manipulate the adults into doing something that the child wants. If it's truly panic, then you might try helping the child back up from the event. What is the first thing that happens when the panic is coming? Is it increased breathing? Sweating? A fear of something? When the child can identify how the panic comes, that may help them get to a point where it can be dealt with.

Undoubtedly, the parents or guardians will have seen evidence of the behavior. They may have some ideas or techniques. For severe cases of panic attacks, children should be evaluated by a psychologist, psychiatrist, or pediatrician.

Discussion Questions

1. What signs of poor coping skills do you see in children? What signs of good coping skills do you see?
2. When you were a child, how did you learn to cope? Who helped you and how?
3. What are some dysfunctional coping strategies?
4. What times or events in your schedule seem to provoke the most anxiety in children?
5. What are some ways you could help kids learn better coping skills?

Helpful Readings and Resources

Reivich, K. & Shatté, A. (2003). *The resilience factor: Seven keys to finding your inner strength and overcoming life's hurdles.* New York: Broadway Books.

Child Anxiety Network, www.childanxiety.net

Reference Notes

The statistic about abdominal pain occurring in 10-15% of children is taken from: Boyle, T.J. (1997). Recurrent abdominal pain: An update. *Pediatrics in Review (18)*, 9, 310-320.

In this chapter:

❖ Curiosity opens up new worlds for kids
❖ Children with curiosity love a challenge
❖ Adults can foster curiosity by nurturing kids' natural creativity

Chapter 7
Curiosity: How
Does That Work?

"Imagination is more important than knowledge."
—Albert Einstein, 1879-1955

TIMMY IS APATHETIC toward everything. He never engages himself, and never throws himself into a project or hobby. Timmy walks around the room, surveying everything, but never trying anything. He frequently complains of being bored. Among the schoolteachers, he is famous for his frequently asked question: "Is this going to be on the test?"

Curiosity is the joy of learning, the thrill of something new. Curiosity cures rigidity, apathy, and grimness.

Curiosity is to have a wide range of interests, and to intrinsically seek knowledge. It includes humor, play, and emotional flexibility. Curiosity is to be wide-eyed with wonder at new discoveries and new images. Curiosity is the joy of learning, the thrill of something new. Curiosity cures rigidity, apathy, and grimness.

This skill cluster helps us with our interactions with others. It gives us hope that we can learn a new thing. It gives us an expectant excitement that each new experience might bring us something new. Curiosity drives our motivation to see life positively and with hope about what we can become. Curiosity gives us motivation to learn about our lives, other people, the world, and our potential.

Figure #8: A Self-Assessment of Curiosity

1. I like to learn about subjects that I know nothing about.
2. I get a thrill from learning something new.
3. I can focus on the journey, rather than the destination.
4. I can live with ambiguity.
5. I am a life-long learner, pursuing a variety of avenues of learning.
6. I like to wonder about things, and ask, "What would happen if..."
7. I can have fun when something goes wrong, because then I get to figure out what went wrong.
8. I view obstacles as challenges.

Children with Curiosity

As with all the skills, adults can determine children's skills through careful observation. Children with good curiosity skills:

- Ask inquisitive questions.
- Like to explore—and actively seek places in which they can explore.
- Create their own adventures.
- Turn routine activities—like clean-up time— into challenging and fun experiences.
- Like to build new things out of construction-type toys.
- Create their own role-plays.
- Investigate new ideas.

- Like to try out new skills and new activities.
- Will experiment with everything.
- Accidentally stumble on topics that spontaneously peak their interest.
- Are open-minded when friends suggest a new game.
- Show flexibility with new ideas and new schedules.

Curiosity teaches us to look at life's situations from different perspectives. This is critical for the development of empathy and respecting diversity. Curiosity helps us care about others because we get the opportunity to learn more about others.

The skills of this cluster are important for motivation and learning. Curiosity helps children make connections between what they know and what they are learning. They are typically intrinsically motivated—they don't need an external threat (the test) or reward (a good grade) in order to do the work. They like learning new ideas and they like learning new activities—simply because they enjoy it.

Some Warning Signs

When children are under stress, curiosity could be the first skill to be left behind. When children are using lots of emotional energy to cope with life, they will tend not to be curious during that time. If the stress passes, their curiosity can come back. If the stress is permanent, they can grow up as wholly uncurious people. The following are some signs indicating that the skill of curiosity is low:

- **Everything is "boring."**
  When children think everything is boring, that could be information that curiosity is poorly developed (on the other hand, it may really truly be that the task is boring). When curiosity is low, children prefer the instant gratification of video games to the adventure of discovery. New challenges are avoided, and apathy sets in.
- **Curiosity becomes recklessness.**
  In a few children, they exhibit a tendency of recklessness—and it may *look like* curiosity on the surface. These children perform dangerous stunts—and risk their own safety and or the safety of others. This kind of thrill-seeking is not curiosity, it's an addiction to the rush of danger. Reckless activity needs to be stopped.
- **Anxiety is high when faced with a new task.**
  Children without the ability to "go with the flow" are troubled by new, unfamiliar tasks. They don't have the capacity to just enjoy the moment, or look forward to the new experience. They worry about trying something new. They frequently make excuses about why they can't do something. The excuses become methods of avoiding something new.
- **Intolerant of ambiguity.**
  Children without the skills of curiosity might want to control things so that they can keep the comfort of their schedule. Rigidity and predictability become critical, because they don't like surprises. They have difficulty with exploring and adventure because they are, by definition, ambiguous and unpredictable.

Curiosity: The Far-Reaching Skill

Of the seven social skills in this book, curiosity may be the skill that comes and goes most often. If the child is stressed, then curiosity goes down. In times of low stress, curiosity goes up.

However, curiosity may be the most wide-reaching skill. In other words, if children have the skill, they'll be more likely to explore the other skills. Curiosity is a skill-set that gets into everything, and can influence every area of children's lives.

> *Curiosity is a skill-set that gets into everything, and can influence every area of children's lives.*

How Adults Can Help

Here are some ways adults can help with the skills of curiosity:

- **Provide opportunities for creative play, creative expression.**
  While not everyone is good at drawing, painting, or sculpture, anyone can creatively express themselves. Look for new and fun ways for children to express their feelings, their hobbies, their interests, and themselves.

- **Help children understand that there is almost never "one right way."**
  There's more than one way to do most things. Encourage children to do new things and think in new ways. When using coloring sheets, what's wrong with coloring people blue? What's wrong with constructing a building out of blocks that will almost certainly fall over? What's wrong with playing a game, and then changing the rules halfway through?

- **Ask kids to help problem-solve.**
  When there is a new rule to make, or a problem to solve, gather children and allow them to come up with the new rule or the solution. Remember, if you do that, you have to live with the result they come up with!

Here's the Point

The benefits of having a society where people are curious means having a society that has the skills of creativity, flexible thinking, ability to view issues from varying perspectives, and solve problems. When we teach children and youth the skills of curiosity, we help them extend their perception of their world and their opportunities. When we teach and foster the development of curiosity skills our young people arc able to explore options, think outside the box, and look from various viewpoints. With lots of curious people, we could make the world a better place for everyone.

✔ Try This

Ask kids *what would it be like if* questions. What would it be like if we had to walk on the ceilings instead of the floors? What would it be like if air was green instead of clear? What would it be like if people only had one eye in the center of their forehead? What would it be like if people could shoot stinky chemicals like a skunk?

Case Study #5: Ricky and Darin

Ricky and Darin are fourth graders, good friends, who are doing a joint project in an inventor's fair. Darin thought it would be fun to create a way to wash hair without getting shampoo in the eyes. So, he explained the idea to Ricky, who said, "fine."

They met to create a complicated shower cap with hoses and flaps. Water would come in through a hose in the front, and exit through a closeable flap in the back. Every time their attempt didn't work, Ricky replied, in a defeated manner, that "it doesn't work." Darin got excited when it didn't work, because then he could figure out how to make it better. Darin worked hard to get the hoses to seal and the flaps in the right spot. Ricky spent most of his time playing with his hand-held video game that he had brought. Darin was engaged and excited, whether it worked or not. Ricky was bored and non-participative. When the time came to show off their invention, Darin talked, in great detail, about the advantages of the contraption and how it worked. Ricky sat quietly, without much interest.

Ricky is an above-average student, in advanced classes. Darin is considered "average" in school.

What's the difference between Darin and Ricky? Who'll do better in school? Who'll do better in life?

Case Study #6: Samantha

Samantha, a school-age care site supervisor knows that curiosity is piqued in different ways for different children, depending on their learning and thinking style.

She put a pile of various pieces of gym equipment in the middle of the floor and invited children to pick and choose what they needed to create a brand new gym game. The children didn't know what the game would be. That was a curiosity smorgasbord for some. Some of the children laughed and got excited and were thrilled about the game starting before even knowing the game. For other children, the "choose a piece of gym equipment" was a bit too loose and random.

Some children appreciated a more concrete, sequential framework. Samantha turned other children loose with a magnifying glass, and they came back with a categorized list of the various forms of dust found around the room. To nurture curiosity, we need to be open and follow children's lead, creating curriculum as we see their interests emerge.

Frequently Asked Questions

Q Aren't kids just naturally curious?

A Yes! However, it is easy for us to allow our curiosity to drain away. The idea of the "one right answer" eats away at curiosity. Some kids receive pressure to think realistically instead of fancifully, and that eats away at curiosity. The pressure of time and "things to do" hinder curiosity. The instant gratification of video games can make exploration and new ideas seem boring by comparison. Our job as care-giving adults can be to nurture the spark of natural creativity, and keep from adding to the ways kids lose curiosity.

Q Is there such a thing as being too curious?

A Probably not. It is a bad thing when curiosity becomes recklessness, or if curiosity moves toward a lack of boundaries or past the level of appropriateness. However, these behaviors are not "too much curiosity" as much as they are a lack of boundaries. Curiosity can be an excuse for lack of attention to long term projects. But this is not "too much curiosity" as much as it is a lack of focus. So, curiosity can deteriorate into many things… but that doesn't mean that curiosity is bad as much as it is a lack of some other skill.

Discussion Questions

1. Try to identify all the times in a day when you use curiosity skills.
2. Do you consider yourself curious? Why or why not?
3. What are the times or places when children in your care have to use the skill of curiosity?
4. What are the behaviors or words used by children that might signify low curiosity?
5. Read the Ricky and Darin case study. What's the difference between Darin and Ricky? Who'll do better in school? Who'll do better in life?

Helpful Readings

The North Central Regional Educational Laboratory's document, *21ˢᵗ Century Skills*, at www.ncrel.org/engauge/skills/skills.htm

Kohn, A. (1993). *Punished by rewards: The trouble with gold stars, incentive plans, A's, praise, and other bribes.* New York: Houghton-Mifflin.

Langer, E. (1990). *Mindfulness.* New York: Perseus Books.

In this chapter:

- ❖ The skill of communication includes speaking clearly, listening, and assertiveness
- ❖ There are levels of listening and communication

Chapter 8 Communication: I Can Listen and Speak Effectively

First learn the meaning of what you say, and then speak.
　　—Epictetus, 55-135 AD

JOANNIE DOESN'T LISTEN. Her eyes glaze over when an adult talks to her. She is an intelligent girl, and she has no other problems getting along with children. But when the staff person is talking, Joannie is somewhere else— dreaming or preoccupied.

The staff is afraid that someday Tony will explode. When he gets angry (which is frequently), he tenses up all over; his face goes red; and sometimes he quivers slightly. But Tony never makes a scene, never has an outburst. He tenses up for a moment, and then pretends the event never happened. He seems to stuff his feelings deep down. He won't talk to anyone about his tense episodes. The staff have spoken to his mother about the problem; she says he won't talk about it, but has been doing it since his grandfather died.

Both Joannie and Tony are displaying different needs for the skills of communication. Joannie has learned not to listen to adults. For whatever reason, she struggles to stay tuned in. Tony, on the other hand, is struggling to process a traumatic event in his life, but won't talk with anyone about it.

A child with good communications skills has aptitudes for listening (Joannie's need) and opening up to talk about a problem (Tony's need).

Communication is a basic human need. When we communicate, we send messages and receive messages. We listen and we talk; we disclose intimate information and we keep secrets; we articulate our needs, and we talk through disagreements.

Communication is a set of skills, including:

- Listening.
- Assertiveness.
- Communicating clearly.
- Knowing when to express and when not to express.
- Knowing when to express secret or intimate thoughts.
- The appropriate expression of emotions, opinions, and ideas.

Figure #9: A Self-Assessment of Communication

1. People usually understand me when I'm trying to make a point.
2. I can argue a point without putting the other side down.
3. I can get my point across, and still show sensitivity when I'm communicating with someone of a different age or different culture.
4. I know when I need to listen intently, and I know when I can listen casually.
5. I know who I can talk to if I need to talk to someone about a problem.
6. When someone else is talking, I'm not thinking about what I'm going to say next.
7. I understand that communication is not a solo activity.
8. I understand non-verbal communication may be just as important as what I say.

Children with Communication

School-age care providers need to be careful observers to gauge the skills of communication. When the adults see themselves as facilitators of social skills, then every interaction can be a time of gentle coaching.

Learning communication skills helps school-age children learn the skills needed to get along with others. Children not only need these skills for out-of-school time, they need these skills for life.

When the adults see themselves as facilitators of social skills, then every interaction can be a time of gentle coaching.

Communication is one of the fundamental processes through which children learn. Communication is the basis for all human interaction. It is important that children understand the connections between what we say, how we say it, what we mean and how we listen to others.

Children with good communication skills will:

- Help children learn about the perspective of others.
- Articulate their acceptance and appreciation of cultural diversity.
- Practice self-awareness skills, talking about what's going on inside.
- Enjoy conversation.
- Follow the ideas of others.
- Ask questions to clarify the conversation.
- Be better at establishing personal boundaries.
- Articulate their needs.
- Clearly express ideas.

Some Warning Signs

One of the primary hindrances to communication today is that the average kid spends three-to-four hours a day watching television and watching video games. The biggest issue is simply the lack of interaction that goes on while staring at the television. When children are watching television or playing video games, they don't get to practice the skills of social interaction. Television is not an interactive activity – and without interaction—there is no communication.

Some warning signs of poor communication include:

- Children don't listen unless they are yelled at or entertained.
- Children don't express their needs.
- They open up to the wrong people.
- They don't open up to the right people.

- Their communication is aggressive rather than assertive.

The skill of communication could be the most fundamental of the skills. Without communication, we would all be in serious trouble. However, it may be the easiest skill to improve. With practice, guided coaching, and a little bit of patience, almost anyone can learn to be a better communicator. And, the more positively we communicate, the better we get at it—it's an upward cycle.

Levels of Listening, Levels of Communication

There are three ways to listen. Each represent a greater intensity of the listening process.

- **Level 1: Keyword Listening**
  This kind of listening is frequently done by adults, particularly when listening to younger children. This level is when you're really thinking about other things, and you're doing other things, but inserting an "uh-huh" in the appropriate place. If you listen at this level, you probably couldn't repeat what the child said. Adults who listen this way listen for keywords like "butcher knife" or "heroin" or something that will jar their preoccupation. If the adult hears an important keyword, they'll be jolted and ask, "what did you say?"

- **Level 2: Occupied Listening**
  At this level, probably the most common form of listening today, the listener listens and

converses, but is also doing something else. The listener is cleaning up, preparing meals, or folding clothes, but listening and talking at the same time.

- **Level 3: Complete Listening**
  At this level, the listener is completely engaged. They listen with their whole body, marking every word. The listener is eye-to-eye with the communicator. The listener not only hears every word, and hears the tone of the voice, but also sees the non-verbals and the body language. This level takes a lot of time and energy.

  We don't have the time or energy to engage in Complete Listening all the time. On the other hand, if we *never* have the time or energy for Complete Listening, that may suggest a problem. The important thing is to know which level of listening the child needs at any given time.

There are three levels of communication also: Autocratic Communication, Straight Communication, and Complete Communication.

- **Level 1: *Positive* Autocratic Communication**
  This level is related to the power that adults have over children. Sometimes, that power is necessary. Sometimes we need to command them, "Get out of the street!" This is Autocratic Communication. If the child is playing in the street, we don't want to sit down in the street with them, and in a fully engaged way, listen to the reasons they are in the street. We want them to get out of the street.

Sometimes we direct children, sometimes we scold them, sometimes we redirect them, sometimes we warn them. Whatever we do that demonstrates a power over them is a Autocratic Communication.

- **Level 1: *Negative* Autocratic Communication**
Autocratic Communication can be negative as well. Sometimes we insult people. Sometimes we shame children for what they've done. Sometimes we argue with other adults and try to score points on them. "You *never* listen to me!" "You're just like your mother!" "This screw-up is your fault!"

    Negative Autocratic Communication is also about power. However, it is point-scoring, blaming, insulting, and shaming. Negative Autocratic Communication has no place in our work with children (Actually, it should have no place in human relationships at all!).

- **Level 2: Straight Communication**
This level of communication is emotionless and straight. "Are you picking up Sally from piano lessons or am I?" "Would you rather play chess or checkers?" In this level of communication, there are no big emotional issues, no contentiousness, and nothing that will get anyone upset. It's everything from "It sure looks like rain," and "Did you watch the football game last night?" to discussing options for the daily schedule.

- **Level 3: Complete Communication**
This level of communication is for

✔ **Try This**

The Telephone Game is a great communication game to play with groups. Of course, the message that reaches the end of the line is inevitably different than the one that was whispered in the first person's ear. The surprise and laughter at the difference between the two is a great way to kick off a discussion about ways to improve the chances that other people will understand us.

---

conversations that are significant or difficult. The communicators look eye-to-eye, and they watch for the tone of the communication, along with what the body language communicates. Complete communication captures all our attention. This level of communication is typically required for resolving difficult issues, conflict resolution, or communicating intimacies.

How Adults Can Help

• **Help them see when communication has failed.**
  Teaching communication means to help children see where communication has failed, especially after real-life communication failures. Then we might ask them, "What could you have said that would have been more effective?"

• **Encourage them to be assertive.**
  Children often need encouragement to know that it's okay to express their needs.

Case Study #7: Tina

When Tina's parents have disagreements, they almost always turn into screaming matches with insults flying in both directions. Her parents often storm off to different rooms—doors slamming and taking hours to cool down. Tina has picked up this negative pattern of communication when she has a conflict with her peers. She responds to interactions by attacking her peers verbally, and then marching off to another place.

What style of communication is she using? What skills does she need to learn to change this pattern of behavior? What steps could adults take to help Tina learn more positive communication?

They need encouragement to tell someone, "I felt hurt when you said that." Sometimes, children simply need the appropriate words. Sometimes they need your moral support.

- **Remind them to listen to each other.**
  Many children need help understanding that communication is interactive—it's not just about talking. Help children see that in hearing a message, body language and tone are important, too.

Here's the Point

Communication, like the other seven skills listed in this book, is a set of skills. Speaking, listening, and assertiveness are part of the skill-set. With a little bit of coaching and some practice, almost any child can be a better communicator.

✔ Try This

Where communication is concerned, non-verbal "speaks" louder than verbal. Try this: tell your group of kids that you are excited to be with them, but say it in a drab, tired tone of voice. Ask them if they think you are: (a) excited, or (b) not excited. Do it again and tell the kids you really want to listen to them, but turn away and look at the floor or something off in the distance while they are talking. Ask the children for examples of how we can both "show" and "tell" the same thing when we communicate.

Frequently Asked Questions

Q **I try to teach positive communication techniques—but nobody talks like that...isn't it a bit unnatural?**

A Any new way of communication is going to feel unnatural at first—when we use complete listening skills and reflective listening skills for the first times—it may feel a bit strange. The more often we use them however, the more natural they become. As children become more adept at expressing themselves—it's a cycle that will reinforce this positive behavior and make it come easier the next time around.

Discussion Questions

1. Was there a person in your life who helped you to be a better communicator?
2. What ways can we limit the use of Negative Autocratic Communication at your site?

3. What are the appropriate times and places to use Keyword Listening? Occupied Listening? Complete Listening?
4. What aspect of communication comes most easily to you? What aspect of communication is most difficult?
5. How might the staff model appropriate listening and communicating?

Helpful Readings

Verderber, R. & Verderber, K. (1998). *Inter-Act: Using interpersonal communication skills.* Belmont, CA: Wadsworth Publishing Company.

Reference Notes

The levels of listening are adapted from M. Scott Peck. Levels of communication adapted from the work of Sherod Miller, Elam Nunnally, Daniel Wackman.

A classic book on communication, still as relevant as ever, is Virginia Satir's *The New Peoplemaking.*

In this chapter:

❖ Community building is about making friends
❖ Community building is the feeling of belonging
   to a group

Chapter 9 Community Building: I Can Make Friends

"On the far-away Island of Sala-ma Sond, Yertle the Turtle was king of the pond. A nice little pond. It was clean. It was neat. The water was warm. There was plenty to eat. The turtles had everything turtles might need. And they were all happy. Quite happy indeed."

—Dr. Suess, *Yertle the Turtle*

YUNG, A KINDERGARTNER, shares the toys he brings from home. When another child starts to cry, he rushes to their side. He sees himself as a part of the group, and he likes to play with a wide variety of children.

Group time seems to drive Anna crazy. Anna wants her needs met, even if everyone else would have to be inconvenienced. She seems to not understand that other people have needs, too.

Community building is the stuff of getting along with others. Friendship, cooperation, and empathy are integral parts of community. Being part of a group is important to all of us. That sense of belonging is facilitated by the skill cluster of community building.

It's important to understand that *community* is more than just having a group of children in the same place. True community is found in the sense of belonging that each member feels. Community is developed through the voices of the membership and opportunity to contribute to the community. Community is about group-ness, and feeling like we are part of the group.

Community is about group-ness, and feeling like we are part of the group.

The skills of this cluster include the ability to:

- Be empathetic.
- Contribute to the group or relationship.
- Cooperate to complete tasks.
- Consider other people's individual differences.
- Be inclusive.
- Generate trust.
- Be kind.
- Draw others into the group.

When children demonstrate community building they will reach out to others, think about the needs of others, and plan for the needs of others. With this skill cluster children and youth can listen and communicate so that friendships are built and maintained.

Children with Community Building

The benefits of this skill cluster contribute in a meaningful way to society as a whole. It is clear that the sub-skills of the skill cluster build on the skill clusters of communication, curiosity, coping, control, and confidence. Children and youth who develop healthy community-building skills will work in cooperative groups. When they have

Figure #10: A Self-Assessment of Community Building

1. I know how to make friends.
2. I understand the give-and-take of friendship.
3. I understand my role in my community.
4. I respect the different opinions of my friends and peers.
5. I recognize when I can meet the needs of another person in my social circle.
6. I care about the feelings of those around me.
7. I know that what is best for the community might not always be what I want as an individual.
8. I try to understand other people's feelings—even if I've never experienced the same issues.
9. I know that every member of the community is equally important.

personal initiative they will also bring others into the process. These children live and work well with others.

Some Warning Signs

- **The Hoverer**

  Hovering is the action of a child floating on the outside of the group of playing children. Hoverers are uncertain about how to join the group. They are not sure if they will be welcomed, not sure how to ask permission to join, or not sure how to read the social situation. Hoverers might finally burst in awkwardly to join the game, but typically by then the group has moved on to something else.

- **The Loner**

  Loners are by themselves. They have no friends, but more importantly, *they show no interest in friendships*. Everyone spends time alone, where they seem to have no playmates, but the loners are always alone, and never seek out kids with whom to play.

- **The Bully**
Bullies are aggressive and overbearing. They seem to show no conscience. They seem to enjoy aggressive games where people get hurt. Bullies want to see themselves as dominant, and the only way they can see themselves as dominant is when other children fear them. These children frame all relationships in an adversarial manner, and don't understand the give-and-take of relationships.

- **The Dominator**
Dominators are kids who seek to control others. They might be benevolent dictators or angry dictators, but their goal is to get others to do things their way. They are bossy or manipulative, but they honestly don't understand why other's don't do things their way. For dominators, they will be friends with someone as long as their "friend" does everything they want. It's "my way or the highway."

Looking to the Future

Children need to understand community to become productive members of society. Without an understanding of community, we risk having a society where self-service reigns and no one takes on the causes of those less fortunate. Without community building, we are a "me society" where each person is only concerned with their own well-being.

✔ Try This

Play charades with feelings. Have a list of feelings written on paper (or better yet, have the kids brainstorm feelings and write them down). Split the group into groups and ask each group to draw a feeling and act it out. Start with *sad* and *mad*. As they get better, you can make it more tricky with *embarrassed*, *hopeful*, and *thankful*. The more complex emotions may require more people and longer skits to present.

Fundamentals for Community Building

Everyone wants a site where kids like each other and get along well. However, it takes some work to build that kind of culture. If the room is cold and sterile, then community building will have an extra challenge. If the adults don't interact with the children, then community building will have a difficult time. (Refer to the *Checklist for Assessing Community Building Fundamentals* on page 127.) This may give you some ideas of what should be in place to maximize the potential for a community building environment.

How Adults Can Help

- **Arrange opportunities for kids to talk to each other.**
  Structure activities where kids have to talk to a bunch of other kids. Ask them to share hobbies, favorite foods, or favorite vacations. Some children need reasons to talk to other children, or they will keep to themselves. Offer many and frequent activities designed to get to know each other and appreciate differences.

- **Recognize that some children need fewer friends than others.**
Some children need a wide variety of friends. Some children need one friend deeply. Children (and adults) vary on how many friends they need and how deeply they need the intimacy.

- **Help kids respect others' needs (without being a doormat).**
Help kids learn to respect other needs, but not by victimizing themselves. Anyone can let other kids have their way. Help kids respect not only their own needs, but others as well. When needs conflict, they can sort it out.

- **Give kids responsibility in the community building process.**
Community building and the accompanying sense of belonging grow as kids are involved. The key is to allow children to have a meaningful role. Community building skills break down when children live in their homes and school as "honored guests" rather than "contributing members." Give children an active role in designing the room, bulletin boards, activities, events, and daily schedule. Incidentally, as children see that they make a difference and that others rely on them, their confidence gets a boost as well.

- **Individually recognize each child's contributions to the community.**
Fill the environment with examples of activities that the group accomplished

together. Make visual reminders of the strengths in our community. Make community building something that is respected and valued in the group.

Here's the Point

Children need the skills of community building to make friends and feel as if they belong to a group. When adults provide some guided opportunities to practice those skills, children can become more capable at building friendships.

✔ Try This!

Draw a chart with all the children in your room down the first column. In the second column, identify who these children have as friends. If you have a lot of groups at your site, identify their "group membership" in the third column. Obviously, these lists will change from day to day. However, it may give you a sense of a child who is not in any group, or the child who has no friends.

Frequently Asked Questions

Q What do we do when group friendships become cliques?

A Cliques are a natural part of relationship development! The stronger the friendship grows, the more the children will have in common with one another. By the same token, the closer they are with some people, the further they will be from others. Cliques are normal and natural and should not be feared.

Now, if the children or youth in the clique use their closeness as a way to devalue others, then this is a different problem. Then the adult has to intervene and find out why they did that, and remind them that this isn't appropriate.

Discussion Questions

1. Do you have hoverers, loners, bullies, or dominators at your site? What can you do to help them?
2. Who were your best friends when you were in elementary school? Why?
3. What might be some activities you can do to facilitate community building?
4. What kinds of formal groups do you have at your site? What informal groups do you have?
5. Make a chart of who's in what group. Are any of the children group-less?

Helpful Resources

Hamilton, J. (Producer). (2002). *Guatemalan cats: A school-age care observation video.* (Available from Sparrow Media Group, www.sparrowmediagroup.com. Comes with discussion guide.)

Schaffer, H.R. (1996). *Social development.* Cambridge, MA: Blackwell Publishers.

Articles at www.loveandlogic.com

Reference Notes

For more on the distinction between "honored guests" and "contributing members," check out Jim Fay's work on teaching children to be responsible at www.loveandlogic.com

Figure #11: Checklist for Assessing Community Building Fundamentals

Environment

Is the environment set up to make the children feel welcome?
- ❑ The space is warm and welcoming.
- ❑ There is a space for conflict resolution.
- ❑ There is an area for parents.
- ❑ The overall sound when children are playing is "enjoyment."
- ❑ Materials are culturally sensitive and reflective of those attending the program.
- ❑ Children and staff have a place to put their belongings during program time.

Is the environment set up to encourage the children to freely explore?
- ❑ Games and activities are available that promote higher-level thinking.
- ❑ There are areas for science, exploration, snacks.
- ❑ Materials and projects reflect the children's interests and developmental level.
- ❑ Materials are plentiful and easily accessible to children.

Community Building: I Can Make Friends

Do the children work together to keep the room clean and safe?
- ❏ There is space for independent work as well as group work.
- ❏ There are games and activities that promote team building.
- ❏ Children are responsible for set up and clean up of room.
- ❏ Rules are created by the children, are phrased in the children's words, and written by the children.
- ❏ Discipline methods are agreed upon and discussed by children and staff members involved with the program.
- ❏ Staff and children meet at the beginning of each year to devise a site handbook. No revisions are made without a discussion and approval of majority (Some issues of administrative policy or safety might need to be dictated rather than approved by a majority.)

Relationships

Do the children feel cared for by staff?
- ❏ Staff know and refer to each child by name.
- ❏ Staff interact heavily with children on a personal level.
- ❏ Children can express their feelings to a staff member and know they will not be judged.
- ❏ Children trust staff–children approach staff for help.
- ❏ Children are heard–staff listen knee to knee, eye to eye.

Are the children encouraged to bring in their talents and share them with the other children?
- ❏ Staff and children are accepting of one another's abilities (or lack of abilities).
- ❏ Staff and children are accepting of one another's ethnicity and culture.
- ❏ Staff share control and leadership.
- ❏ Staff encourage and support exploration.

Do the children consider their friend's feelings while playing a game or during a conversation?
❑ Children feel valued by peers.
❑ Children have empathy with other children (not just their friends!).
❑ Staff assist children with conflict resolution without taking control of the situation.

Are parents cherished as partners?
❑ Parents are greeted when entering and leaving the program.
❑ Parents, staff and children are asked for their input about the program choices, services and activities.
❑ Staff engage in conversation with parents.
❑ Staff are able to recognize and identify members of child's immediate family and important adult figures.

Experiences

Are children involved in planning their schedules in the SAC program?
❑ Children feel competent and take risks.
❑ Children feel comfortable asking questions.
❑ Field trips are child-centered and children assist in directing them.
❑ Children know the routine.
❑ Children have choices.
❑ The site elects a committee of representatives to meet monthly and discuss issues regarding site.

Community Building: I Can Make Friends

Are the children able to play games, or work on a task together, and use skills of cooperation to make it successful?

❏ Activities are offered on a daily basis that incorporate teamwork.

❏ Children are not grouped by age, grade, skill level, or gender.

❏ Children are encouraged to discuss and handle interpersonal conflicts on their own (staff supervision or coaching is available if required).

❏ The site institutes a "buddy system." Children cannot leave the room without their buddy.

❏ Children are not involved in competitive activities where an actual winner is awarded a prize.

Are the talents of families and community members an integrated part of the program experience?

❏ Community outreach volunteers are part of the program.

❏ Family members are invited and encouraged to participate in field trips and events.

Do the staff have a thorough understanding of their vital role in the development of children?

❏ Staff have paid time to plan activities.

❏ Program experiences are designed to give children opportunities for success.

❏ Staff intentionally plan activities to develop social skills.

In this chapter:

❖ Conflict resolution is being able to talk through a conflict

❖ Conflict is a natural part of relationships; dealing with conflict is a requirement in life

Chapter 10
Conflict Resolution:
I Can Negotiate
Through a Problem

"We must learn to live together as brothers or perish together as fools."
—Martin Luther King, Jr., 1929-1968

PHIL IS AN AGGRESSIVE second-grader. He is quick to hit others, quick to have a temper tantrum, and quick to escalate an interaction into a hostile encounter. The other school-age children are afraid to play with him because he plays too rough.

> *A conflict-free existence is not possible, so, in order to live together, we need to be able to resolve conflict.*

When Sabrina gets in an argument with one of her third grade peers, she usually starts off okay. But before the negotiation goes very far, Sabrina begins to yell at her friends and then stomps off in anger. She loses her temper quickly, and she gets too frustrated in the process.

Human beings argue and have conflict. It is natural, normal, and a part of human existence. A conflict-free existence is not possible, so, in order to live together, we need to be able to resolve conflict. Conflict resolution involves a wide range of skills, capacities, and perceptions.

When we use the word *conflict*, we are limiting the definition to interpersonal disagreements. We are not talking about violence, assaultive aggressiveness, or issues of physical safety. Interpersonal conflict and disagreement are normal and natural. Aggressiveness and violence are not natural or normal, and should never be tolerated.

Aggressiveness and violence are not natural or normal, and should never be tolerated.

Some children (and adults) have only one conflict resolution skill: power. They believe if they can exert enough power, their conflict will "go their way." Consequently, if they don't get their way, they simply ramp up the power. This is an unfortunate lack of conflict-resolution skills.

The skills of conflict resolution include:
• Understanding that aggression is undesirable.
• Negotiation.
• Problem-solving.
• Compromise.
• Keeping one's temper in check.
• Coping with one's own feelings.
• Thinking about solutions.
• Understanding one's own perspective and being able to conceptualize others' perspectives.

> ### Figure #12: A Self-Assessment of Conflict Resolution
>
> 1. I can distinguish an attack on me from disagreement with my opinion.
> 2. I can hold my anger in check while I search for solutions to a problem.
> 3. I can see how my perspective factors into the problem.
> 4. I can react without defensiveness.
> 5. I can visualize win/win scenarios.
> 6. I can respect others' opinions even if they differ from mine.
> 7. I do not see victory in overpowering or controlling anyone.
> 8. I can compromise and be okay with that.

Children with Conflict Resolution

Children who have the skill of conflict resolution have these kinds of attitudes and behaviors:

- **They aren't afraid of conflict.**
  They approach problems without fear. While few people enjoy conflict, those with this skill aren't afraid of it either. They can approach it without letting it fester, without letting it become bigger than it needs to be. When conflict is not dealt with, it often festers and becomes worse, and other problems get attached to it. Those with the skill of conflict resolution can approach the conflict at an early stage.

- **They can pick their battles.**
  Children (and adults) with the skill of conflict resolution don't have to fight every battle.

Some can be left alone, and they go away. Some conflicts, when left alone, can fester. Those with the skill of conflict resolution know the difference.

- **They will respect one another's opinions and differences.**
  Those with the skill of conflict resolution know that everyone has their own opinion. Sometimes, those different opinions will bump heads. People with this skill don't have to feel that their opinion is valid, and everyone else's opinion is "stupid." Those with this skill know that many opinions are valid.

- **They tend to try for win-win solutions.**
  Children with conflict resolution skills are less interested in "getting their way" and more interested in "everybody getting their way." When everyone gets their needs met, it is a win-win solution.

- **They know there's more than one side to every story.**
  As kids grow older, they realize that there's more than one perspective on events. They realize that the summary they got from one person may differ from the summary they get from another person.

- **They manage anger.**
  Anger is a normal part of life (although violence is not!). Children with conflict resolution skills will have outlets for managing their anger and understanding their physical reactions to anger.

Some Warning Signs

- **Interpersonal conflict becomes aggressive quickly.**
  When disagreements become shouting matches quickly, that could be evidence that a child has poor conflict resolution skills. Rapid escalation can be a dangerous situation.

- **Issues are framed adversarially.**
  Some children, when faced with an ambiguous situation, immediately frame the situation as adversarial. If Freddie wants a particular toy, and Charles is leaning up against that toy as he is doing something else, Freddie is faced with an ambiguous situation. Is Charles "keeping him from the toy" or is Charles oblivious to the toy and doesn't care if Freddie uses it? Aggressive children believe the former. Aggressive children frame issues adversarially—"Charles has my toy."

- **Interpersonal conflict becomes about persons, not issues.**
  People have opinions, but they are not defined by their opinions. Some children (and adults) believe if their opinion is questioned, then their integrity is automatically questioned.

- **A paranoid avoidance of conflict.**
  The opposite of engaging in conflict too quickly is having a paranoid avoidance of it. Being frightened of interpersonal conflict suggests that the skill of conflict resolution is low (unless safety issues enter the situation—then, it becomes a different issue). While no one enjoys conflict, being unable to function when conflict is present is also a danger sign.

Conflict-Prone Kids

Aggressive children start conflicts quickly and easily; however, they are not necessarily "looking" for a fight. Each of us, when faced with an ambiguous social situation, generate a list of alternatives. Aggressive children also generate a list of alternatives, but the list is much shorter for them. So everyone—including aggressive children—view violence as a last resort. The problem is that aggressive children can only generate a short list of options, whereas non-aggressive kids can generate a long list of options. Aggressive children frame social situations adversarially, and have a much poorer repertoire of skills.

The problem for conflict-prone kids is not that they are looking for fights. Their problem is that they have difficulty thinking through complex social situations. They don't understand what's going on, and so they react adversarially and aggressively. Aggression is still their last resort—but they quickly exhaust all their other skills for dealing with problems.

Conflict-prone kids need help understanding social situations, how kids feel, and that other kids are not out to get them. They need a better understanding of relationships, interactions, and social situations. They need better social skills.

How Adults Can Help

Adults need to be careful how they teach the skills of conflict resolution. Imagine that we see a rapid escalation of a disagreement between Scott and Freddie. Scott is clearly taking the power position, and is ratcheting up the power he brings to the situation. Freddie is shrinking quickly. At the current rate of escalation, in a few minutes, Freddie will give up everything and Scott will take everything. Scott is rapidly becoming the bully, and Freddie is rapidly becoming the victim.

There is a danger here. If we swoop in and rescue Freddie, putting Scott "in his place," we will be reinforcing Freddie's victim mentality. So, if we swoop in and rescue Freddie, then Freddie will be more of a victim next time, waiting for an adult to intervene. Scott will be more of a bully next time.

What we need to be concerned about is, "how do we keep Freddie from becoming a victim in this relationship, and how do we quell Scott's tendency to become a bully?"

The adults then, need some more complex skills than an aerial rescue. Perhaps the adult could give some kind of moral support to Freddie. Perhaps the adult could stand behind Freddie as Freddie articulates his perspective to Scott. Freddie, not the adult, is the one who needs to stand up to Scott.

Teaching conflict resolution takes some significant teaching time, and then monitored follow-up of their resolution techniques.

Never let them "fight it out." But neither do you create destructive victim and bully roles for the children. Coaching, mentoring, and gentle help can keep participants on the road to mutual conflict resolution.

Teaching conflict resolution takes some significant teaching time, and then monitored follow-up of their resolution techniques. Peer mediation and mentoring by older children is helpful to the process.

✔ Try This

During group time, give children an issue or have them pick an issue. Let them promote one side, and after awhile, ask them to switch sides. This helps them to see that all issues have another side, and it's okay to respect it even if you don't agree with it. Even if we don't agree, we can at least understand the other perspective. Children learn to do this when staff ask them to explain the other person's side. It can be hard to do that in the midst of a conflict, so children will need to practice it.

Here's the Point

There are many programs and curriculums that teach conflict resolution. However, the process of conflict resolution must be more than "this month's program." Conflict resolution needs to be lived—discussed, talked about, and practiced. The skills of conflict resolution could be a positive part of any program.

Frequently Asked Questions

Q I've done a conflict resolution curriculum in my program, and it failed. What did I do wrong?

A The skills of conflict resolution build on other skills. In order for positive conflict resolution skills to be demonstrated—there must be community building going on and an active sense of community present. Children need to understand anger-management techniques and perspective. However, that being said, situations are not failures if the children learn from them.

Just because the children might not have handled a conflict in the most productive way, that doesn't indicate complete failure of the process. Take the time to process this with the children in the hopes that this experience will further the process the next time.

Q How can you respond when parents teach their children that "if someone hits you, you hit them back?"

A The children will have to be instructed that "rules are different here." They may use that rule at home, but "here, things are different." You can explain what the rules are at your site, and you can do that without devaluing their parent. The parent, also, will need to be instructed that "this is the behavior we expect when the child is here." What the parent and the child talk about at home is something you can't control—nor should you. But you can control the rules that are present at the site. If the parent cannot live with those rules, you can recommend that they try some other child care centers in your area.

Discussion Questions

1. What are your techniques for managing your own anger?
2. What techniques have you seen be successful for children's anger management?
3. How do children learn empathy? Have you seen examples of children who take another's point of view?
4. Does your site need conflict-resolution training? Are you ready for it, or are there other skills to work on first?
5. How might you get older children involved in the process of teaching conflict resolution to younger children?

Helpful Readings

Coloroso, B. (2003). *The bully, the bullied, and the bystander: From preschool to high school—how parents and teachers can help break the cycle of violence*. New York: HarperResource.

The Peace Education Foundation (www.peaceeducation.com) has useful conflict resolution curriculums.

Reference Notes

What we have called "conflict-prone kids" is from research by Ron Slaby.

TEACHING SOCIAL SKILLS

Teaching Social Skills

In this chapter:

❖ How to find out what social skills kids need
❖ The difference between a skill deficit, a
  performance deficit, and a self-control deficit

Chapter 11 Determine the Needs

"If you judge people, you have no time to love them."
—Mother Teresa, 1910-1997

There are three ways to teach social skills. For the best possible experience, children need to be taught in all three ways.

Direct teaching of social skills: This occurs when we sit the children down and teach the skill, just as a classroom teacher would teach an academic subject. We might use a commercially prepared curriculum, an activity book, or our own ideas. We might talk about the skill, see a skit, watch a video, or engage in role plays. The point is that this is formal time where the adult orchestrates a lesson about a social skill. Chapter 12 provides more detail about direct teaching.

Integrated teaching of social skills: This occurs when the adult plans art, gym, or other activities, but adds a social skill component into the activities. The activity might be a game, an art project, or any kind of group activity, but learning a social skill is a part of the process. The children might not even realize that they are learning a social skill while they do the project. The group may or may not discuss the fact that social skill instruction played a part of the activity. Integrated teaching involves intentional planning on the part of the facilitator. Chapter 13 provides more detail about integrated teaching.

Situational teaching of social skills: This is when social skills are taught in the natural setting as children experience interaction. Situational teaching is to teach conflict resolution when a conflict breaks out. It is to teach communication when there has been a misunderstanding. It is to teach coping when something difficult has happened. Situational teaching is to grab the teachable moment. Chapter 14 goes into more detail on situational teaching.

But before you do any of that, for maximum effectiveness, you need to determine the children's needs.

What Exactly Do They Lack?

A classroom teacher, in preparing for tests, would never just impulsively guess, "I think the kids need extra help with spelling." The teacher, through careful observation, watches what the class is excelling in, and what subjects the class would need help with. If the teacher gives them extra help in spelling, when they *really* need extra help in math, the teacher has wasted the class' time, and done no good.

A social skills teacher follows the same process. Through careful observation, we need to determine exactly what the needs are—and then design experiences that meet the need.

Through careful observation, we need to determine exactly what the needs are—and then design experiences that meet the need.

Observe the children while they play and interact, and then ask these kinds of questions:

- What skills are lacking?
- Why are the children lacking a skill?
- Are there some skills present in all the children?
- Do some children demonstrate a skill sometimes, but not other times?

When you see that children aren't showing a skill they need, there are three possibilities of "what's going on."

1. There might be a *skill deficit*. The child does not know the necessary skill.
2. There might be a *performance deficit*. The child knows the skill a little bit, but applies it poorly.
3. There might be a *self-control deficit*. The child knows the skill, and could perform it adequately, but the lack of another skill (such as managing their anger) interferes with the successful performance of the skill.

Skill Deficit

A *skill deficit* means children are deficient in the skill itself. They simply don't know the skill.

Kevin is a fifth grader who sits by himself most of the time. He doesn't look sad or act like he's been rejected, he just finds his own chair and sits down. Sometimes he reads a book, and sometimes he just stares. When the group goes outside, he walks laps around the equipment. Adults talk to him sometimes, because they are worried that he's depressed. However, Kevin talks freely, sometimes excitedly, with staff, usually going into detail about the new video game he is playing at home with his dad. When other children ask him to join a board game or fill out one side of a team, Kevin often responds with, "I can't right now, I'm thinking about Age of Empires." When he is asked a question or included in a conversation, Kevin looks thoughtful, but usually gives short, one-phrase answers and bows out. Kids say they like Kevin, but most have given up on trying to get him involved. Kevin has a community building skill deficit.

The following clues could help you determine if there is a skill deficit:

- No other emotions seem to play a part in the incident (they are not angry, etc.).
- The child has never shown the skill.
- In all settings and situations, the child does not show the skill.

When a social skill deficit is present, for maximum effectiveness, the children first need direct teaching. They need the structured, intentional teaching so they can learn the ins-and-outs of the skill. It can then be followed up more effectively by integrated and situational teaching.

Performance Deficit

A *performance deficit* is a faulty knowledge of a social skill. They kind of, sort of, know the skill, but they perform it poorly. Like a beginning tennis player who hits the ball into the net 90% of the time, a performance deficit is seen in a child who has just learned a skill, and can't apply it well.

Simon is learning about control. In the past, he has been prone to reacting physically and verbally to other children. His favorite phrase is, "*They* did it first." Through direct teaching, Simon stopped hitting other children back. Instead, he now runs out of the room or kicks chairs. He also returns fewer put-downs with bigger put-downs. When a child antagonizes him, Simon no longer throws a punch immediately. Instead, he yells across the room to the teacher, "Did you hear that??! If he says that again I'm gonna punch him! No matter what! He deserves it!" Simon has shown some gains in the skill of control, but he still has a long way to go.

The following clues could help you determine if there is a performance deficit:

- No other emotions seem to play a part in the incident (they are not angry, etc.).
- The child sometimes has shown the skill, or parts of the skill.
- The child begins to show the skill, and then it falls apart.

If children show a performance deficit, they need to practice. They need role-plays and closely monitored coaching. They need a healthy dose of situational teaching—so they can practice the skill in a real situation with an adult nearby.

Self-Control Deficit

A *self-control deficit* means that children know the skill, but before they can use the skill, another emotion hijacks the child. The self-control problem might be anger, it might be fear, or it might be a dislike for the other person.

Rhonda is trying to get Sally to understand why she didn't cheat at the game. Rhonda explains, but Sally doesn't understand. Before Rhonda can clarify herself, she gets frustrated and has a temper tantrum. So, to a casual observer, Rhonda didn't communicate well. However, a careful observer will see that Rhonda never had a chance to use her communication skills because her anger got in the way.

The following clues could help you determine if there is a self-control deficit:

- Emotions are high, such as anger or fear.
- You've seen the child use the skill in non-emotional times.

With a self-control deficit, there is a need to teach the other skills that have led to the skill interference; so for Rhonda's case, she needs to learn coping skills—specifically, anger management.

A Diagnosis is Not a Cure

If you go into the doctor with a headache and nasal congestion, the doctor might pronounce the diagnosis, "you have a sinus infection!" At that point, do you thank the doctor and walk out? No—you get antibiotics to cure the infection. The diagnosis is not the same as the cure. The diagnosis must come first, so the correct cure can be applied—but then the cure comes second. First diagnosis, then application of the cure.

The purpose of assessing children is so that we might effectively provide the appropriate social skills training.

Sometimes beginning social skill teachers confuse the diagnosis with the cure. They'll observe a child carefully, and then pronounce, "the child has poor confidence skills," and then they think they're done. But the adult isn't done, because no "cure" has been applied. Doctors only diagnose so that they can effectively apply the cure. In the same way, we assess children only to effectively apply an educational intervention.

So, if the adults only diagnose and assess children, then they are using their observation skills unethically. The purpose of assessing children is so that we might effectively provide the appropriate social skills training.

Figure #13: How to Observe a Child

Here are some sample questions to help you become a more effective observer of a child. You don't have to answer every question; the questions are simply meant to spark your insight. Through careful observation, we can get insight into the behavior of children and their social skill needs.

Recall what you know about the child.
- What is the child's family make-up?
- Who are their friends?
- What are their likes and dislikes?

Observe the child in the program environment.
- How does the child act in a large, open space?
- How does the child act in a small space?
- How does the child act in a quiet space?
- How does the child act in a creative play space?
- How does the child act in a construction zone space?
- Does the child become easily engaged or roam about?
- Does the child take cues from the environment (e.g., the child knows that a quiet space is for quiet play)?
- Does the child respond to environmental changes in a positive way?

Observe the child's relationships—the interactions with others:

- How does the child interact with peer groups of two or more?
- Is there a time when the child's involvement with a group becomes limited or stressful for the child? Does the size of the group change the behavior of the child?
- How does the child do in mixed age groupings (with those older or younger)?
- Does the child know how to approach others?
- Does the child know how to engage in friendships?
- Does the child know how to maintain friendships?
- Is their play with others limited in any way?
- Is the child assertive, or is the child a follower?
- Does the child listen and respond to others?
- Does the child need intervention and support from adults? If so, how does the child respond to this support? When is the support needed?

Observe the child's experiences—the structured activities:

- How does the child interact and become involved in group experiences?
- Does the child prefer to play alone?
- Is the child willing to share?
- Is the child willing to participate fully?
- What is the child's attitude toward the experience (boring? aggressive? engaged?)?
- What does the child's behavior in an experience tell you about the child's perceptions of their own skills?

Here's the Point

If you want to teach social skills most effectively, you need to understand if there really is a social skill deficit, or simply that some other emotion is getting in the way. Careful observation, with some tools, will help narrow our list of choices so that we can get the "biggest bang for the buck."

The next step is teaching the social skills!

Frequently Asked Questions

QWhat about role modeling?

A Role modeling is all well and good. However, contrary to popular belief, it is not very effective at teaching positive skills. One reason could be that children and youth with low social skills also have a lower ability to take in information through role modeling. Most often, the very children we want to learn from us aren't even watching. To effectively use role modeling it's best to role model by asking the children to "watch what I do" as you do the skill in a real setting. Then, sit down with the child afterwards and ask, "What did you see?" and help the child understand what you did and why.

Discussion Questions

1. Give an example of a skill deficit that you have seen in a child recently.
2. Give an example of a performance deficit that you have seen in a child recently.

3. Give an example of a self-control deficit that you have seen in a child recently.
4. What might be some unethical uses of diagnosing social skills?
5. Why is it important to try to determine whether you're looking at a skill, performance, or self-control deficit?

Helpful Readings and Resources

Benson, P. (1997). *All kids are our kids: What communities must do to raise caring and responsible children and adolescents.* San Francisco, CA: Jossey-Bass Publishers.

Knapczyk, D. & Rodes, P. (2001). *Teaching social competence: A practical approach for improving social skills in students at-risk.* Verona, WI: Attainment Company, Inc.

Helpful readings at www.developkids.com

Reference Notes

The three deficits were identified in: Cartledge, G. & Milburn, J.F. (1995). *Teaching social skills to children and youth: Innovative approaches.* Needham Heights, MA: Allyn and Bacon.

In this chapter:

❖ Teaching social skills through curriculum and lesson planning
❖ The ESP approach for teaching social skills

Chapter 12
Direct Teaching of
Social Skills

"Be gentle with the young."
   —Juvenal, 55-127 AD

AFTER YOU HAVE determined the children's
needs, the next step is to teach the skill. As we've
already said, there are three ways to teach social
skills:

- *Direct teaching*: where you sit the children
  down, and you are the teacher, and you
  start a mini-class on a social skill. You have
  prepared a lesson plan that will help the
  children understand the knowledge and skills
  associated with the social skill.
- *Integrated teaching*: in this form, you're doing
  some activity—but you have intentional
  designs to teach a social skill while this
  activity is going on. It's using the activity to
  teach a social skill—and the children may or
  may not know they are learning a social skill.
- *Situational teaching*: this is the teachable
  moment—it is teaching conflict resolution
  when there is a conflict, and teaching
  communication when people aren't
  understanding each other.

Direct teaching is most effective for skills that are unfamiliar to the children. The skills the children lack most glaringly are the skills that would be the prime targets for direct teaching. Direct teaching gives children an introduction to the skill, the language of the skill, and the uses and applications for it.

The ESP Process for Direct Teaching

The three-step process, Explain-Show-Practice (ESP), can be used to plan a direct teaching lesson on any social skill.

1. *First, **explain** the skill to the children.* You introduce it, explain it, help them understand why it's important. You might engage them in a discussion about the skill, and what it looks like if someone doesn't have the skill. Some examples might be:
- Videos
- Act it out
- Draw it out on a dry erase board
- Give a mini-lecture

2. *Second, **show** the skill in action.* Kids need more than to just know about the skill. They need to see the skill in action. Show the children what interactions look like when the skill is present. You could:
- Perform a role play
- Conduct a puppet show
- Show a video of people using the skill
- Show a movie or TV episode where the skill is present (or not present)

3. *Third, practice the skill.* Allow the children to practice the skill with one another. You might put them in pairs and give them a situation to act out. You might want to have children write skits about children that have the skill or don't have the skill. You could:

- Rehearse it as if it were a play
- Role-play or write a drama
- Use workbooks
- Make up a song
- Have a debate
- Write poems

Benefits of Direct Teaching

Having the right vocabulary: When children have the language to talk about an issue, it becomes easier for them to internalize the issue. When children lack the appropriate language base to think about social skills, they can misunderstand and misapply the concepts.

Actively practicing the skill: Children need opportunities to practice any new skill. This can be done through role-plays, puppet shows, or creating a song or story together. With enough practice time, success emerges.

✔ Try This

Have the staff role-play a situation. It's up to the children to be the director—and to yell "cut" when they see staff not using the appropriate skills in their role-play. Then the staff can lead a discussion about "what went wrong" and "what could we have said that would have shown the appropriate skill."

Applying the skill in new situations: This is called *transfer of knowledge*. We learn the information in one place, but then we apply it in a brand new place. Contrary to popular belief, this is not an automatic process! Children (and adults) who "learn" something, can frequently fail to use it in situations where they need it!

Teachers need to give lots of help to the transfer process—asking children how they might use a skill in *this* situation, or *that* situation. Transfer is more likely when we teach in different places; teach with different people; use a variety of teaching styles; work with the parents and school-teachers; and help the children learn how to self-evaluate.

Breaking the skill down into subskills: When we teach directly, it's easy to make a list of the sub-skills of each skill. For example, we could break *Communication* down into several subskills. *Listening* might be one of those subskills. *Listening* could be further divided into patience, waiting your turn, etc. You might want to involve the kids in that "breaking-down" process, asking them for actions that match each word.

✔ Try This

For example: If the rule is to treat each other with kindness—then we build the language of kindness by breaking the skill down. Have the kids brainstorm what they think kindness is and is not....

KINDNESS IS NOT	KINDNESS IS
Name calling	*Asking permission*

Here's the Point

There's no mystery to the direct teaching of social skills. You Explain the skill, Show the skill, and Practice the skill with them. When children are deficient in a skill, direct teaching could have the most impact. Of course, it must be followed up with integrated and situational teaching.

Frequently Asked Questions

Q Our schedule is such that there is not a lot of time for group time... so direct teaching becomes difficult to put in the schedule. Do we absolutely have to do direct teaching to be successful at social skills?

A You can still make progress teaching social skills through situational teaching and integrated teaching. In fact, if you had to give up one of the three types of teaching, you would probably want to give up direct teaching. So, if you don't have direct teaching (but you do situational and integrated), you will have success. But you will probably have more success if you include direct teaching. The bottom line is, you can't do everything that children need for their lives regarding social skills, so do what you can.

Discussion Questions

1. What might be some ways you could start a direct teaching process?
2. Have you ever been a participant in a class teaching social skills? What was it like?
3. What are some other ideas for the direct teaching of social skills?
4. If you had to start today, which of the seven social skills would you begin with?
5. Research suggests that when social skills are enhanced, academic grades improve. Why do you think that is?

Helpful Readings

Elias, M., Zins, J., Weissberg, R., Frey, K., Grenberg, M., Haynes, N., Kessler, R., Schwab-Stone, M., & Shriver, T. (1997). *Promoting social and emotional learning: Guidelines for educators.* Alexandria, VA: Association for Supervision and Curriculum Development.

In this chapter:

❖ Integrated teaching is teaching social skills while you're doing another activity

❖ Kids may or may not know they're learning social skills with integrated teaching

Chapter 13
Integrated Teaching
of Social Skills

"You cannot teach a man anything; you can only help him find it within himself."
  —Galileo, 1564-1642

TO REVIEW: there are three ways to teach social skills: *direct teaching*, where we intentionally and actively teach the skill. *Integrated teaching* is where we teach the skill while we're doing something else. *Situational teaching* is teaching the skill at the moment when the child needs it the most.

In integrated teaching, we choose an activity–perhaps an art project, or a game, or a sports activity–and we pair it with a social skill that will be used during that activity. Integrated teaching can be done with almost any activity. In integrated teaching, you identify the social skills kids will need for the activity, and then after the activity, you can engage them in discussion about it. In integrated teaching, children may or may not know they are learning social skills!

Integrated teaching is best used with social skills that the kids partially know. Maybe the

> *In integrated teaching, we choose an activity… and we pair it with a social skill that will be used during that activity.*

children know the skill, but have difficulty using it in all situations, or they forget to use it when they need it. This is the best time to use integrated teaching. Integrated teaching helps kids to transfer their knowledge to the situations where they need it.

The Two Questions: Setting Kids Up for Success

One of the goals for integrating teaching is to set children up for success. We know they need a particular skill, so we bring it to their awareness as we begin the activity.

If we help them understand the skills that they will need before they play, everyone will have a better experience.

Children with low social skills have a low awareness of environmental cues. In other words, they don't always connect what's happening in their environment to needing to change their behavior. So, for example, if you have a multi-age group playing dodge ball, the fifth graders with low social skills won't know that "I have to be more careful when I'm throwing the ball at the second grader." If we help them understand the skills that they will need before they play, everyone will have a better experience. And, most importantly, the children will be practicing a social skill.

When setting kids up for success, we need to explore two questions with the children. These two questions are the critical part of integrated teaching. If you explore these questions with the children, there is a good chance children will learn the skill. If you neglect these two questions, there

Case Study #8: Lois

Lois is the lead provider at the school-age care site. About 15 kids are participating in the after-school art lesson. The craft calls for lots of paper cutting, paper folding, and some gluing. Lois sets out 10 scissors, and 2 glue bottles.

Lois could have set out 15 scissors and 15 glue bottles. But she has been noticing more conflicts around the issues of patience and sharing. She wants to teach the kids some better skills in those areas. She intentionally set out less scissors and glue bottles so that she could teach them about sharing.

As Lois explains the art project, she sets out the 10 scissors and the 2 glue bottles. She reminds them that they'll have to share the glue and the scissors. She asks, "How will we be successful sharing the scissors and glue?" She engages them in a short discussion about that. The kids give suggestions like, "We'll have to be patient," and "We can't all have the scissors and glue at the same time." Lois asks the next question, "When you're waiting for the scissors or glue, what will you do?" Again, the kids offer ideas like, "Talk quietly with someone else," "Work on the folding," or "Start a new project."

After the craft is over, Lois debriefs with them. She asks what it was like to wait for scissors and glue. She commends them where they did well and identifies the skills she saw.

Lois needed to teach skills of patience and sharing. She indeed taught those skills, in the context of an art lesson. The children were able to practice those skills, and many of them did not even know they were practicing social skills!

is a good chance children will **not** learn the skill, and the children will have missed an opportunity.

What behaviors (or skills) will you need in order to be successful? Before the activity starts, you'll want to explore what they're going to need. So, if you have overanxious fifth graders who are going to play dodge ball with a multi-age group, you'll want to sit them down before the game. You'll say, "We're about to play dodge ball with a group of kids from second grade to fifth grade. You are the oldest kids playing, and we want everyone to have fun and no one to get hurt. What will you need to do to be successful with that?" The fifth graders will say a variety of things, but you can key in on their comments, "being careful when I throw a ball at a second grader." You might even hear someone say, "It's not about winning, it's about having fun." The important thing is that you ask the question, and they give the ideas. You want them to come up with the ideas. If the fifth graders don't get it, and you get the sense that they are not going to careful, you should probably have them sit out or play their own game.

The second question that is part of the process is: *What will you do when you need the skill?* This is not a redundant question. Fifth graders will be all too happy to suggest "be careful when throwing a ball at a second grader"... but they won't realize that this means them! This phenomenon, well known in educational research, is called *inert knowledge.* It is when the fifth grader believes that "kids" should be careful when throwing balls at the second graders, but don't know that *I* should be careful when throwing a ball at the second graders. That's why we ask the second question.

So you would want to ask the fifth graders, "when you're about to throw a ball at a second grader, what will you need to think?" Wait for answers like, "Throw softly," or "Don't throw as hard as I can," or something like that. This will give kids the opportunity to think through their own personal strategies.

Steps to Preparing a Lesson

There are four steps to plan an integrated teaching lesson:

Step 1: Choose the social skill or the activity. You might think of a social skill you want to practice, and then match it with an activity. Or, you might think of an activity you want to do, and then identify the skills they need to complete the activity successfully. Either way, choose the activity you want to lead and the social skill you want to teach. What are the goals? Is the social skill the most important goal, or the activity?

Step 2: Plan the activity and the lesson. Plan the activity as you normally would. Then plan the social skill component. How can you teach the skills? Will you need to simply remind them of the skills, or will you need to model it for them? Can you make a change in the activity to accentuate the learning of the social skill, as Lois did in the case study?

Step 3: Do the activity. If it's an art project, show them a completed project. If it's a game, tell them how to finish the game. As you introduce the activity, engage them in conversations about the social skills they'll need to finish successfully. It's important that you not simply *tell* them the skills they'll need; instead, ask the children for ideas on how to have a successful activity. Then, ask the children what they will do when they need that skill. You may need to demonstrate the social skills they'll need. As the activity progresses, you may need to remind children of the skills they'll need—especially if you see the children forgetting.

Step 4: After the activity, debrief with the children. Identify and celebrate the accomplishments of the group. Recap the learning. You may want to allow the children to say what they liked best about the activity. If the activity deteriorated, ask them what should be done differently next time?

Figure #14: Integrated Teaching Lesson Plan

	Choose the Social Skill	Choose the Activity
Step 1: Choose	What social skill do you want to teach?	What activity do you want to do?
Step 2: Plan	What skills will we need to teach?	How will we carry out the activity?
Step 3: Do the Activity	Don't forget the two questions: 1. What will it take to be successful? 2. What will you do when it comes time to use that skill?	
Step 4: Closure and recap	How did it go?	

Here's the Point

Integrated teaching is a powerful way to teach social skills. It takes a small amount of time, and a willingness to engage the children in some discussion before an activity, but it has huge payoffs. In integrated teaching, we set children up for success as they engage in an activity.

Frequently Asked Questions

Q Does it take a lot of time to do integrated teaching?

A No. It can add as little as 45 seconds to the lesson to discuss ways to be successful and what they will do. If their skills are low, or the behaviors you expect from them are complex, you may have to stop and practice those skills—which will take a little longer. Forty-five seconds is a small price to pay to teach social skills and set kids up for success.

Discussion Questions

1. Name a few of the activities that you have done over the past few days. What social skills are a natural part of the process of that activity?
2. In what other ways can we set children up for success?
3. Why is it better to ask children "What skills will you need?" rather than just telling them the skills they'll need?

4. In the case study, Lois had 15 children, but only put out 10 scissors and 2 glue bottles. How would the experience have been different if she would have put out 15 scissors and 15 glue bottles?

5. What steps would you need to take at your site to start a process of integrated teaching of social skills?

Helpful Resources

Garbarino, J. (1995). *Raising children in a socially toxic environment.* San Francisco, CA: Jossey-Bass Publishers.

Charlie Steffens and Spencer Gorin's book, *Learning to Play, Playing to Learn*, is full of great games and activities for integrated teaching.

For more integrated teaching ideas, check out Zoom Games on the PBS Kids website at http://pbskids.org/zoom/games/

Reference Notes

The concept of *inert knowledge* was first identified by Alfred North Whitehead.

In this chapter:

❖ Taking advantage of the teachable moment
❖ Being a social skills coach

Chapter 14
Situational Teaching
of Social Skills

"Don't limit a child to your own learning, for he was born in another time."
—Rabbinical Proverb

TWO BOYS ARE ARGUING about the rules for a game. Each one thinks the other is cheating. The adult facilitator knows the boys and knows they are capable of solving this problem, but their voices are getting louder, and accusations of cheating are getting worse. The leader stoops down next to them, and quietly suggests that, perhaps they could brainstorm a list of solutions, rather than just trying to convince the other boy of his idea. The boys agree; within minutes they are listing the ways they could resolve the situation—some of the ideas are workable, and some are silly. A few minutes later, the leader returns and asks if they had come up with a solution to solve their problem. The boys look at her with a puzzled look and ask, "What problem?"

Situational teaching focuses on the teachable moment.

If direct teaching is teaching with a lesson plan, and integrated teaching is teaching with another activity, then situational teaching focuses on the teachable moment. Situational teaching is coaching, mentoring, and giving suggestions. Situational teaching is to teach conflict resolution when there is a conflict, or teach listening when kids aren't listening. Situational teaching is to gently intervene into the situation and remind kids of the skills they need to be successful.

If situational teaching is not a follow-up to the direct and integrated teaching, very few children will learn social skills. Situational teaching is critical to the learning process. In the heat of the moment, kids (and adults!) who have incomplete social skills will not think to use their best skills. They may need some gentle coaching... some reminders to use those skills *right now*, in this current situation.

Intervening in Situations

When we say that staff should *intervene* in situations, we mean that adults should gently enter the situation just enough to help it along in a positive way. Adults shouldn't impose themselves where they're not needed. They shouldn't burst on to the scene as judge and jury. They shouldn't intrude into a situation where they're not wanted (unless, of course, there are safety issues involved).

A football coach can't jump into the game and play for the participants.

Adults need to be careful, because kids will automatically see the adult as having the power to "set things right." They will try many different strategies to get the adult to take over for them. The adult, however, needs to see themselves as a coach, not as a player.

Case Study #9: Anthony

Anthony is a fourth-grade boy who could be described as being "wound pretty tight." He's very articulate with a vocabulary well above his grade level. Anthony is always perfectly dressed, and his hair is always neatly combed with a part on the side. The precision of his appearance hints at the precise way he works, plays and acts. He is on medication for ADHD.

Anthony's quick smile dissolves into an impatient frown if his mom or dad don't arrive precisely on time to pick him up. While he waits, the lines on his forehead get deeper every time he glances at his oversized digital wristwatch. When his parents finally arrive, usually only five or ten minutes late, Anthony grumpily berates them. Explanations like "bad weather" or "backed up traffic" don't help him let go of his frustration.

Late pick-ups turned out to be an opportunity to teach Anthony coping skills. Staff taught Anthony simple self-talk and breathing exercises. When it gets close to pick-up time, instead of looking at his watch, Anthony takes a deep breath and says, "Even though my parents might be late, I'm okay." As it turned out, this kind of a pre-emptive strike helped Anthony relax quite a bit. If his parents do end up being late, Anthony breathes and says, "Even though I'm nervous, I'm okay," or "Even though I'm angry, I'm okay."

With some self-talk and some deep breathing, Anthony learned how to relax more effectively. By helping Anthony recognize and deal with his frustration, the staff have helped Anthony develop a skill that will help him the rest of his life.

Eventually, staff might be able to help Anthony not just cope with his late pick-ups, but enjoy them. Eventually, Anthony may see the late pickup as "more time to play" or "more time to spend with my friends." But the staff wisely chose "coping" as the skill to help build, because that's where Anthony was.

A football coach, for example, can't jump into the game and play for the participants. The coach can only give suggestions, advice, or ask questions, and then the coach has to leave, so that the participants can finish the play.

Here are some hints about intervening:

- *Intervene after careful observation.* In situational teaching, as with all aspects of social skills, it's critical to be a careful observer. You might intervene before a conflict occurs, during a conflict, or after it has occurred, but your judgment needs to be informed by careful observation. Stay long enough to give them a boost.

- *Intervene with questions, not answers.* Typically, it is better if the children realize the problem on their own, rather than being told. A well-placed question might facilitate more effective learning. "Maybe we both had different ideas on the rules of the game," is an important revelation when the children realize it.

- *Intervene gently, not intrusively.* It's helpful if the adult can be gentle in their approach. This reminds everyone that a crisis need not occur. It can also remind children that their problem is for them to work out—that they shouldn't wait for an adult to swoop in and solve their problem. The children need to work it out, but the adult will be available if needed.

Case Study #10: David

Third-grader David doesn't like waiting for others. He gets impatient and frustrated when he's ready and he has to wait (although paradoxically, the other children often wait for David). David is impatient when waiting for directions, and gets frustrated when the staff have to repeat directions. He frequently screams out "Shuddap!" when the staff are trying to get children's attention.

When it was David's turn to help lead a game during gym time, David found himself in front of a group of children who weren't paying attention. Before he could scream at the group, the staff person, sitting next to him, whispered "Do you have any suggestions for how to get the group's attention—so we can get started with the group game? David, was caught off guard, and said, "maybe we should tell them to be quiet." The staff person asked David, "What do you think would happen if we just started shouting at everyone? Would they listen? Would they even hear us?"

The staff person, knowing David had poor skills in transition times, tried to help him see the consequences of his actions. Perhaps the staff person could help David come up with some creative ways to get the group's attention. By engaging David in a rational discussion before he lost his temper, the staff person was able to teach David to look at his own behavior and measure its effectiveness.

- *Intervene, but try to avoid taking sides.* Children (and adults) with poor conflict resolution skills see conflict as a win-lose issue. In other words, they can only conceive of an end goal as "one person wins and the other loses." They will often wait for an adult to come in and do that—make one person the winner and one the loser. When we take sides, we reinforce that mindset, and in so doing, we don't help their conflict-resolution skills. Sometimes, of course, the adult needs to take sides. But when possible, try to help them find a way out of their issue without relying on an adult to be the judge and jury.

When to Intervene

When should you intervene in a situation? It's a little bit more of an art than a science, but here are some general guidelines.

- *Intervene when things are escalating.* When kids are having a disagreement, for example, and the voices are getting louder and sharper. When things are escalating, it's a good time to insert yourself into the situation. Sometimes a gentle word might be enough. Sometimes you may have to remind them about "the skills we've been practicing." Sometimes you might have to give them some hints or helps.

- *Intervene before they lose control.* When we allow tempers to flare and children to lose control of themselves, then we've doubled our problems. So, when possible, intervene before things get out of hand. If you're too late, sometimes a cooling-off time is helpful. But don't just send them apart from each other and think you've solved the problem. You'll need to bring them back together (after they've cooled off) to work through the issue.

- *Intervene when one person is being victimized.* When possible, don't allow kids to slip into the roles of *bully* and *victim*. When they play out those roles, they reinforce the roles, "I guess I really *am* a victim." When roles are reinforced, it makes it more difficult for victims to stand up for themselves next time. It's a vicious cycle. The victim needs to stand up to the bully. And, the victim will usually need the moral support of the adult in order for this to happen.

- *Intervene when things have been festering.* If kids can't solve the problem, it's time for an adult to help out. Sometimes people get stuck, and they can't think their way out of a situation. An adult who can give the situation a little boost can help move it on its way to resolution.

- *Intervene when conflict starts to spread.* If children start to get other kids involved in the conflict, it's time to intervene quickly. When more kids get involved in the conflict, and groups begin to take sides, then the adults suddenly have a host of new problems. When possible, intervene before it starts to spread.

Situational Teaching of Social Skills

- *Intervene if you know the kids' skills are too low.* If the conflict or situation is too complex for the kids who are involved, you can do a preemptive strike. You may want to help them see the upcoming conflict. You may want to ask them what skills they will need if they get stuck. Obviously, you're guessing at their competence level… but for some children, it's better to be preemptive than wait until they lose control.

Being a Social Skills Coach

A situational teacher is a social skills coach. The coach jumps in when needed, but then jumps out when they're not needed. The coach can't "do" the skill for the child—the child needs to learn and practice the skill. Good social skill coaches have a number of characteristics:

- Good coaches are good observers. They carefully watch what goes on. They are present for the children when they need it.
- Good coaches recognize that mistakes can be a good teacher. With a little help from the adult, the child can think through the mistakes and learn.
- Good coaches see themselves in a partner role. A social skills coach will desire to be the children's partner in learning social skills; sometimes an active partner, sometimes a silent partner, but always a partner.
- Good coaches focus on strengths. Every person has strengths and weaknesses, but a good coach will build off of strengths—what the child already knows.

- Good coaches help the players identify their own needs. A social skills coach can help the children see when and how they need a skill, rather than simply telling the children what they need.

Here's the Point

Situational teaching means to intervene in the teachable moment. Good situational teachers have all the skills of a good coach. They can intervene smoothly in order to gently redirect the situation. Just a few calm words may be enough to boost the children into using better skills.

Frequently Asked Questions

Q When tempers flare, what can adults do to help children "cool down," in a quick and teachable way?

A If you know a child has a quick temper that frequently flares, its helpful to have a plan for that child. When tempers flare, the child's brain is emotionally "hijacked." It's like a switch in the brain, making it suddenly difficult for the child to think clearly. One quick idea is to signal the child to "take two" which means "take a quick walk to the drinking fountain." The movement of the walk combined with the refreshing water might help the brain un-hijack. Eventually, the goal would be to teach the child to notice the signs of a temper flare before the flare occurs, so the child can "take two" without a drinking fountain and without an outburst.

Discussion Questions

1. Identify some teachable moments you have seen over the past few days (whether or not you have intervened).
2. What's the difference between a harsh imposing of the adult into the situation, and a gentle intervening? Why is the "gentle intervening" better?
3. How can adults learn the skills of being a social skills coach?
4. Who are some children at your site with whom you would intervene quickly? Who are some children with whom you would not immediately intervene?
5. In the case study of impatient David and his problem with waiting, the staff were able to intervene before David lost control. Why do adults often wait until *after* there is problem behavior—even when they know the problem is coming?

Helpful Readings

Pierangelo, R. & Giuliani, G. (2000). *Why your students do what they do and what to do when they do it.* Champaign, IL: Research Press Company.

Vernon, A. (1989). *Thinking, feeling, behaving: An emotional education curriculum for children.* Champaign, IL: Research Press Company.

Conclusion

"You miss 100% of the shots you don't take."
—Wayne Gretzky, Hockey Player and Philosopher

A SCHOOL-AGE CARE provider is a facilitator of positive development, a teacher of social skills. Adults in out-of-school time programs orchestrate a myriad of activities, games, and supervision… but in everything, they facilitate positive development in children. That's the key that should be the center of the work of adults in school-age care. They facilitate the positive development of children.

Teaching social skills is the gift we can give to children (and to society!). We can be a powerful influence on the development of children—if we are a little bit intentional. School-age care is a premier place to teach social skills to children and youth. Too many children are growing up without those peaceful living skills—and lives get wasted when society overlooks the teaching of social skills.

A school-age care provider is a facilitator of positive development.

Teaching social skills is a little like exercise. It's less important what you do, and more important that you just do something. That's like the teaching of social skills. Don't worry if you don't have all the information, or don't have all the answers. Just do it. It costs very little, but there is a possibility of huge payoffs.

One activity probably won't teach a social skill perfectly. It doesn't have to. But a pattern of social skill building activities can—and does—teach the skills that will last a lifetime.

That's our mission.

Index

About the Authors

Jim Ollhoff

Jim is a writer and college professor. Jim's academic background includes training in education, family studies, developmental psychology, social psychology, and systems theory. Jim's academic interests are the process of discovery in anxious systems, effective management from a complexity perspective, leadership, strategy, and adult learning. He teaches courses in the areas of family studies and management. Jim is married to Laurie, and they have one delightful son, Dominic. For fun, Jim reads, writes, bakes unusual breads, and studies martial arts.

Laurie Ollhoff

Laurie's academic background includes work in child development, education administration, program development in out of school time, social skills, and program assessment. She has worked as a school-age care provider, and has been a classroom teacher in middle schools, and an art teacher K-6. Laurie has a passion for the positive development of children. In her spare time, Laurie paints, sculpts, volunteers as an art specialist at the local school, spends time with Jim and Dominic, and plays with her cats. Laurie speaks frequently at conferences and consults with school age programs.